SEQUEL TO SEATTLE

Canada, the GATS and the future of Health Care

Matthew Sanger

Canadian Centre for Policy Alternatives

National Library of Canada Cataloguing in Publication Data

Sanger, Matthew
    Reckless Abandon: Canada, the GATS and the future of health care

Includes bibliographical references and index.
ISBN 0-88627-260-2

1. Medical care—Canada. 2. Insurance, Health—Canada. 3. General Agreement on Trade in Services. 4. Medical policy—Canada. 5. Insurance, Health—Government policy—Canada. 6. Free trade—Canada. I. Canadian Centre for Policy Alternatives. II. Title.

RA449.S35 2001   362.1'0971   C2001-900343-9

Printed and bound in Canada

Published by

Canadian Centre for Policy Alternatives
Suite 410, 75 Albert Street
Ottawa, ON K1P 5E7
Tel 613-563-1341   Fax 613-233-1458
http://www.policyalternatives.ca
ccpa@policyalternatives.ca

Acknowledgements

Many thanks to Scott Sinclair and Bruce Campbell for their constant support and encouragement, even as I missed our original deadlines! I benefited immensely from Scott's insights and good humour at every stage of writing this book. I am grateful for helpful information and comments from Diana Bronson, Cynthia Callard, Tony Clarke, Ellen Gould, Ron Labonte, Mike Luff, Stan Marshall, Mike McBane, David Price, Jane Stinson, Michelle Swenarchuk, Steven Shrybman and Ken Traynor; and for a final editorial scrubbing by Ed Finn. I take full responsibility for any errors of fact or interpretation.

This research was funded by supporters of the Trade and Investment Research Project, in particular the Canadian Federation of Nurses, Canadian Union of Public Employees, National Union of Public and General Employees and Public Service Alliance of Canada.

Contents

Chapter 4
Causes for Concern: Implications for Specific Health

Chapter 5
Conclusion and Recommendations

Figures

Tables

Summary

This report assesses the implications of the General Agreement on Trade in Services for Canada's health care system. It examines both Canada's commitments in the existing GATS agreement, which came into effect in 1994, and the agenda of the current round of GATS negotiations, known as GATS 2000, which are informally scheduled to conclude by the end of 2002.

Our report is the most detailed assessment to date of how the GATS affects Canadian health care. Yet it is not a comprehensive analysis, which would require detailed examination of the regulatory environment for each specific health-related service in all 14 federal/provincial/territorial jurisdictions. Instead, the report provides an overview of GATS implications for health care, then assesses its impacts for health insurance, hospital services and home care. The analysis of these three critical health services suggests the full range of GATS impacts. But one of the report's goals is to demonstrate that more comprehensive exploration, and full public debate, of the potentially profound implications of the GATS for the Canadian health care system are urgently required.

The Minister of International Trade and Canadian trade negotiators clearly do not welcome such a debate. The minister and his trade officials have repeatedly and emphatically assured Canadians that health care will not be affected by the GATS. Such assurances are, to put it charitably, misleading. This report finds that Canada's health care system is *already* more exposed to GATS rules than Canadians have been led to believe and that the GATS 2000 negotiations threaten to further extend coverage of health care.

Given the sweeping scope of many GATS provisions, and their fundamental incompatibility with the principles and practices governing the Canadian health care system, Canadians should arm themselves with a healthy dose of skepticism when they are told that our government has ensured that Canadian health care is fully protected from GATS impacts.

Health Care at Home, Market Access Abroad: Canada's conflicting agendas

Our report confirms concerns that Canada's trade policy is driven by narrow commercial interests which conflict with the public interest in maintaining a universal publicly funded health care system.

In section 2.3 we review the federal government's strategy for promoting exports of Canadian health services. Based on highly unreliable growth projections, the government's official strategy document focuses entirely on expanding market access for Canadian telehealth services. The "barriers to market entry" identified in this document include foreign regulatory measures designed to maintain professional standards; guard against malpractice and fraud; contain costs; and ensure patient privacy and confidentiality. To identify these measures as "barriers to market access" for Canadian telehealth exports is to target in other countries the public tools we require to maintain the integrity of our own health care system. If this agenda is allowed to influence Canada's negotiating objectives at the GATS, we may participate in the dismantling of our health care system. Even Canada's commercial health services corporations acknowledge there would be "a price to pay" for pursuing their agenda.

Canada's export promotion policy is not only inconsistent with our domestic policy commitments. It also conflicts with our obligation under the International Covenant on Economic, Social and Cultural Rights to uphold the right to health in our international relations. Targeting the health policies of our trading partners is inconsistent with the obligation "to respect the enjoyment of the right to health in other countries." Furthermore, Canada's willingness to use its negotiating leverage in pursuit of the commercial objectives of health services exporters contradicts the obligation to prevent private businesses and other "third parties" from violating the right to health in other countries.

The priority Canada gives to expanding markets for telehealth is of particular concern because telehealth applications cut across the full range of health care services. Any trade rules which apply to telehealth as a group could restrict how governments provide and regulate home care, diagnostic services, health information, and other vital components of the our health care system. There is a danger that telehealth could be covered by GATS rules developed in the e-commerce negotiations which are being fast-tracked in the GATS 2000 negotiations.

Causes for Concern: GATS implications for health care

Sections 3 and 4 of this report examine the health care implications of the GATS. We find that federal government reassurances that health care will not be affected are highly misleading.

Important features of our health care system are already exposed to the full force of the GATS rules. It is alarming that in the previous round of negotiations Canada passed up all opportunities available to it to explicitly shield these exposed services from the GATS rules. The report uncovers an error in Canada's listing of health insurance, which reinforces fears that our representatives at the GATS table have been negligent in discharging their duty to protect health care.

Our examination of GATS implications for specific health services finds good reason to be concerned that it will interfere with Canada's capability to maintain and renew Medicare:

i) Incredibly, Canadian health insurance is already fully covered under the GATS national treatment and market access rules. Fundamental protection for public health insurance is undefined and strictly limited in scope. This exposes Canada to the threat of trade challenges that restrict options for health reform:

- GATS rules restricting monopolies (Article VIII.4) already expose to challenge any future expansion of Medicare coverage to encompass health services currently covered by private health insurance, e.g. home care, and pharmacare.
- The risk of high compensation costs could deter any such policy initiative.

(ii) Other services related to health insurance – including data-processing and on-line information retrieval – are also already fully covered by the GATS national treatment and market access rules. These rules would allow a foreign-owned commercial insurer operating in Canada to assert a GATS right to process Canadian health insurance claims and records remotely from outside the country.

- This would reduce the cost to U.S. health insurers of expanding their operations in Canada.

- By removing claims processing from Canadian jurisdiction, it would also make it very difficult for provincial health ministries and other regulators to protect the privacy of patient records and ensure that such
health information is used for ethical purposes.

iii) Hospital support services are likely already subject to
the GATS national treatment and market access rules. This
restricts the ability of hospitals and regional health authorities to "contract in" food, laundry or janitorial services:

- Hospitals and regional health authorities would be
vulnerable to a GATS national treatment challenge,
charging that "contracting in" modifies the conditions
of competition against foreign-owned service providers.
- The federal government would be required to ensure
that hospitals or regional health authority reversed
"contracting in" decisions, or, if they did not, to provide compensation to the governments of adversely
affected foreign service providers.

iv) Medical services in hospitals are protected from the
GATS general rules as long as they are provided on a non-
commercial basis and not in competition with private health
facilities (Article 1.3). This protection is undermined by
Alberta's legislation to permit public funding of private for-
profit hospitals, and by more limited revenue-generating
activities in other provinces. The combination of the GATS
general rules and Canada's NAFTA obligations, which
could also be triggered by the Alberta legislation, could
expose our health care system to a potentially ruinous trade
challenge. If the federal government does not act against
Alberta, the NAFTA national treatment rule could be trig-

gered, preventing the federal government from intervening to prevent similar practices in other provinces.

- Once *any* foreign-owned health corporation has used
  NAFTA to gain access to public health funding, the
  GATS most favoured nation (MFN) rule could extend
  the rights of *all* foreign-owned corporations. Most
  dangerously, it would enable them to claim a right to
  receive the same level of subsidy as is provided to
  any other foreign-based health corporation.
- Moreover, the GATS principle of "modal neutrality"
  could be invoked by a for-profit hospital corporation
  to assert a right to the same level of public subsidy
  for treating Canadian patients outside the country
  (e.g., in the United States) as is given to commercial
  hospitals providing the same service to patients in
  Canada. A successful trade challenge could give a
  virtually unlimited number of commercial hospitals
  beyond our borders a claim on Canada's public funding for health care, exposing Canada to trade retaliation and potentially overwhelming the capacity of
  provincial and federal governments to contain costs
  and regulate the quality of care.
- While this chain of events may appear unlikely, the
  logic of Canada's trade obligations makes them possible. Since WTO trade tribunals have shown a readi-
  ness to apply GATS rules as forcefully as possible, it
  is imperative that Canada take steps to protect our
  health care system *before* it is the subject of a trade
  challenge.

v) While professional home care services are not covered
by the national treatment and market access rules, the general GATS rules already apply.

The MFN provision equips foreign-owned providers to accelerate the commercialization of home care in Canada. MFN requires that the most favourable treatment given to any foreign service or service provider be given "immediately and unconditionally" to *any and all* foreign services or service providers. This allows all home care providers to claim a right to the most advantageous deal given to any single foreign-based providers.

The MFN obligation and the modal neutrality principle could restrict governments' ability to regulate telehealth applications in home care:

- Conditions for public funding of telehealth applications — e.g., video assessment and monitoring of home care patients — could have a differential impact on commercial providers from different WTO member countries.
- A successful MFN challenge would give foreign-owned companies providing remote telehealth services from outside Canada (cross-border supply) the same access to public funds for home care as foreign-owned companies based in Canada (commercial presence).

vi) Canada can expect to face considerable pressure to extend GATS coverage of home care, which is among the fastest growing health services and is an area of intense commercial interest. Extension of market access and monopolies rules to home care would restrict options for health reform:

- The market access rules (article XVI.2(e)) could prevent governments from providing public funding only to not-for-profit home care providers.

- The monopolies rules (article VIII) could deter governments from directly providing home care services that were previously contracted to commercial providers.
- These restrictions would limit the ability of governments to provide publicly funded home care services in the most cost-effective manner.

The GATS and the Future of Health Care

Based on the analysis summarized above, the report recommends a number of practical steps the Canadian government should take to ensure that Canada's GATS obligations do not compromise our ability to maintain a universal, publicly funded and regulated health care system:

- *The Canadian government must unequivocally affirm that safeguarding Canada's health care system will take precedence over securing market access for Canadian exports. It must disavow the dangerous illusion that Canada can gain access to other countries' markets for health services without ever granting access to the Canadian market in return.*

- The Canadian government should oppose any initiative to extend GATS coverage of telehealth services as a group, and it should ensure that the negotiations on ecommerce and telecommunications do not affect health services provided electronically or by other means.

- The Canadian government should conduct a systematic and comprehensive assessment of the health impacts of our commitments under the existing GATS agreement.

- *The Canadian government should raise the issue of the "governmental authority" exclusion during the GATS 2000 negotiations so that its meaning is clarified, and it is made fully effective. Amendments to this provision will be required to ensure that mixed public-private services, including health care, are fully excluded from the GATS.*

- *Canada should insist on a general exception for health care, which applies to all WTO members and will not be targeted in future rounds of negotiations, Because of the diversity of national health care systems, any such exception must be self-defining (as is the existing general exception for national security measures).*

- Agreement on explicitly excluding health care from the scope of the agreement, either through amendments to article I.3 or by means of a new general exception, should be a precondition for agreeing to any further commitments in the GATS 2000 negotiations.

- *Canada should also use every opportunity available to it to explicitly shield health care from the GATS rules. In addition to excluding health care services from the scope of the agreement, our negotiators should enter explicit exceptions and limitations to all GATS commitments which may affect any health care services.*

- *Special action is needed to safeguard Canada's ability to modify public health insurance in accordance with domestic policy priorities and without fear of provoking a GATS trade challenge. Canada must invoke GATS Article XXI to modify its schedule of specific commitments in health insurance. It must enter a limitation which explicitly shields public health insurance from these commitments. In order to preserve the ability to extend Medicare, Canada must also change the status of its commitments in commercial health insurance from "bound" to "unbound." This would remove the danger that private corporations could challenge future changes to Medicare which may affect their ability to provide commercial health insurance.*

- *In the GATS 2000 negotiations, the Canadian government should make clear its opposition to extending coverage of health care services. It should:*

  - *oppose negotiations on rules regarding non-discriminatory domestic regulations, which would extend the reach of the GATS far into areas of domestic policy including health policy and working to eliminate the provisional application of the restrictions on domestic regulations contained in article VI; and*

  - *insist on maintaining the bottom-up features of the GATS, and oppose so-called "horizontal" negotiations which could extend GATS rules to health service by stealth, i.e., without requiring them to be positively listed.*

Beyond the GATS: Health as a "global public good"

Strengthening Canada's health care system requires pursuing an international agenda. This agenda should not only ensure that trade agreements do not infringe upon the ability of citizens to democratically determine how they will support the health of their societies. It must also strengthen international mechanisms for addressing health issues that transcend national borders.

- *Canada should join leading health experts and support concrete efforts to build international mechanisms for addressing health as a "global public good."*

- *There are practical steps the Government of Canada can take to help initiate this ambitious agenda. The revision of the WHO International Health Regulations is one modest opportunity for Canada to advance global health. By supporting the competence of the WHO in determining legitimate health risks involved in WTO trade disputes, Canada would contribute to strengthening the enforcement of the International Health Regulations.*

- *Canada must also work on a larger canvas to support other nations in meeting the health needs of their citizens. It should support efforts to build a more balanced international economic order in which commercial interests no longer take precedence over human rights, environmental protection, income redistribution, and other health-determining conditions. In addition to strengthening the WHO and other international health organizations, Canada should support initiatives to counterbalance the authority of trade tribunals with more accountable forms of global governance.*

- *The primacy of human rights, including the right to health, should be assured in practice as well as in theory. To this end, Canada should support establishing a mechanism for resolving complaints of violations of nations' obligations under the International Covenant on Economic, Social and Cultural Rights. The federal government should also review its export promotion and trade policies to ensure that they are consistent with its obligation under the Covenant to "respect the enjoyment of the right to health in other countries, and to prevent third parties violating the right in other countries..."*

These steps would better support the values that underlie our health care system than is possible within the framework of the GATS agreement and the commercial principles which it advances. Continued public pressure will be needed to convince our government that the GATS must be fundamentally reformed.

Chapter 1
Health, Trade and GATS:
Perspective and Scope of this Report

There is growing recognition — in Canada and internationally — that trade and health and their respective regulatory frameworks are closely linked. Obviously, the health of a population is affected by, and may influence, the course of global economic integration. Moreover, exporters and international investors may view certain health policies and regulations as restricting their commercial opportunities. And market-opening international trade and investment rules have increasingly come into conflict with public policy measures to promote health.

Not long ago, international trade and investment agreements were considered to be of purely commercial significance. Now these agreements — which are among the principal policy instruments shaping global economic integration — are recognized as having important implications for the health of citizens.

Access to AIDS drugs. Disposal of PCBs. Asbestos exports. Plain packaging of cigarettes and other measures to reduce tobacco consumption. Regulation of gasoline additives. Food safety. These are some of the diverse instances in which trade rules have been used recently to threaten or overturn health policies.

The link between trade and health was even alluded to by Prime Minister Jean Chrétien in a much-publicized paper presented to a group of world leaders concerning the challenges of globalization:

"Canada's approach is to support greater policy coherence at the international level, to address not only the economic, but also the social, environmental, health and cultural consequences of globalization. All governments will have to meet the challenge of building an international agenda that is coherent, and governance structures that are transparent and that engage civil society domestically and internationally."[1]

Not surprisingly, however, there is no consensus on the nature of the connection between trade and health. Proponents of more liberalized trade and investment generally claim that the overall health impacts are positive: over the past 25 years increased trade and investment has raised productivity levels and has led to higher average incomes and better standards of living — including better health status – for everyone in all but the poorest countries. Some critics question the basic premise of this argument: there is no conclusive empirical evidence that liberalized trade and investment, and not other factors, are responsible for raising average incomes and standards of living worldwide. Furthermore, trade liberalization may be linked with dramatic increases in income inequality both within and among nations; and inequality in health outcomes has increased in tandem with income inequality. Some critics are also concerned that existing patterns of economic growth will themselves cause detrimental health and environmental effects.[2]

These macro-level positions are inadequate for understanding the specific health impacts of modern international trade agreements such as the GATS. Health is more than a function of one's level of income, although economic and social conditions – including the distribution and level of employment and income — are important determinants of the health of a population. Also, trade agreements are of more than commercial significance. Since the Uruguay Round, international trade negotiations have addressed a wide range of "non-tariff barriers," including regulatory measures; trade obligations which restrict these measures may affect health independently of any economic impact of liberalized trade.

This study focuses on the implications of the GATS for the Canadian Medicare system and health care services. First, however, the following section clarifies the analytical perspective of this study, by situating these specific concerns within the broader context of the relationship between international trade and health.

The right to health in international law[3]

The international community has recognized individuals' right to health since the Universal Declaration of Human Rights was adopted in 1948. While the extent of this right and the specific obligations it places on nation states are a matter of debate, the Declaration and subsequent international instruments are consistent in defining health broadly to include mental and physical well-being and in recognizing the significance of socio-economic factors which influence health.

Article 25.1 of the Universal Declaration of Human Rights (UDHR) affirms: "Everyone has the right to a standard of living adequate for the health of himself and of his family, including food, clothing, housing, and medical care and necessary social services." This right is further elaborated in the International Covenant on Economic, Social and Cultural Rights (ICESCR), in which Canada and other signatories recognize "the right of everyone to the enjoyment of the highest attainable standard of physical and mental health." (see Table 1).

The Covenant, which has been ratified by 142 states (including Canada, but not the United States), has its legal

Table 1: Health as a Human Right

Universal Declaration of Human Rights (1948), Article 25:

(1) Everyone has the right to a standard of living adequate for the health and well-being of himself and of his family, including food, clothing, housing and medical care and necessary social services, and the right to security in the event of unemployment, sickness, disability, widowhood, old age or other lack of livelihood in circumstances beyond his control.

International Covenant on Economic, Social and Cultural Rights (1966), Article 12:

(1) The States Parties to the present Covenant recognize the right of everyone to the enjoyment of the highest attainable standard of physical and mental health.

(2) The steps to be taken by the States Parties to the present Covenant to achieve the full realization of this right shall include those necessary for:

a)   The provision for the reduction of the stillbirth-rate and of infant mortality andfor the healthy development of the child;
b)   The improvement of all aspects of environmental and industrial hygiene;
c)   The prevention, treatment and control of epidemic, endemic, occupational and other diseases;
d)   *The creation of conditions which would assure to all medical service and medical attention in the event of sickness.*

foundations in the Charter of the United Nations and the Universal Declaration of Human Rights. It maintains the broad definition of health adopted in the Universal Declaration and in addition specifically recognizes environmental and industrial factors affecting health. The right to health "must be understood as a right to the enjoyment of a variety of facilities, goods, services and conditions necessary for the realization of the highest attainable standard of health, " according to the United Nations Committee on Economic, Social and Cultural Rights.[4]

> ...the drafting history and the express wording of article 12.2 acknowledge that the right to health embraces a wide range of socio-economic factors that promote conditions in which people can lead a healthy life, and extends to the underlying determinants of health, such as food and nutrition, housing, access to safe and potable water and adequate sanitation, safe and healthy working conditions, and a healthy environment.[5]

In its own domestic policy Canada has adopted a similarly broad approach to health. Although its provisions apply exclusively to health care services, the Canada Health Act acknowledges that health is about more than health care and that other factors and policies are important in determining health. Its preamble recognizes that

> ... Canadians can achieve further improvements in their well-being through combining individual lifestyles that emphasize fitness, prevention of disease, and health promotion with collective ac-

> *tion against the social, environmental and occu-*
> *pational causes of disease, and that they desire a*
> *system of health services that will promote physi-*
> *cal and mental health and protection against dis-*
> *ease;*[6]

While recognizing a broadly defined right to health, the UN Committee on Economic, Social and Cultural Rights specifies the steps governments must take to realize this right. The Covenant obliges states to not only respect and protect the right to health but also to actively work towards fulfilling it by facilitating, providing and promoting the conditions necessary to enjoy health and well-being.

In recognizing the constraints that limited finances and other resources may place on national governments, the Covenant provides for the "progressive realization" of the right to health. Certain "core obligations," such as the right of access to health facilities without discrimination of any kind, are of immediate effect. Other obligations require States to take "deliberate, concrete and targeted [steps] toward the full realization of the right to health." Progressive realization, in the words of the Committee, "means that States parties have a specific and continuing obligation to move as expeditiously and effectively as possible toward the full realization of article 12." It further stipulates that "there is a strong presumption that retrogressive measures taken in relation to the right to health are not permissible." [7]

For the present study it is especially relevant that the Committee interprets the obligations of states under the Covenant to extend to their international relations in addition to their domestic policies.

> *In order to comply with their international obligations in relation to article 12, States parties have to respect the enjoyment of the right to health in other countries, and to prevent third parties from violating the right in other countries, if they are able to influence these third parties by way of legal or political means ... States parties should ensure that the right to health is given due attention in international agreements and, to that end, should consider the development of further legal instruments.[8]*

Private businesses are included among the "third parties" referred to above. The Committee notes that all members of society, including the private business sector, "have responsibilities regarding the realization of the right to health." Because only States party to the Covenant are accountable for compliance with it, they "should therefore provide an environment which facilitates the discharge of these responsibilities" by businesses and other third parties.[9]

Canada and other signatories are required to regularly report to the Committee on steps taken to implement its commitments in the Covenant, including the right to health. However, there is no United Nations mechanism for compelling a signatory nation to comply with its commitments in the Covenant. With very few governments prepared to support a proposal for a complaints procedure for Covenant rights violations, the Committee can only issue opinions and reports which are not legally enforceable, although they may have political influence.

In this regard there is a marked discrepancy in the development of international human rights law and international trade law – where the decisions of trade tribunals reach deep into areas of domestic policy and are enforced by economic sanctions.

This creates an anomaly in international law. Human rights, including the right to health, are founded in the Charter of the United Nations and the Universal Declaration of Human Rights which take precedence over conflicting obligations in any other international agreements, including trade agreements. Yet, without a complaints procedure and effective means of ensuring compliance with the right to health, there is no legally enforceable means of asserting its priority.

Trade-Creep in Health Policy

Over the past decade there have been numerous instances in which trade obligations have been employed to challenge, and in some cases overturn, health measures introduced by Canada and other nations (see Table 2 for a summary). These instances demonstrate the consequences of vesting authority in trade tribunals to enforce their interpretations of novel trade obligations which apply to a sweeping range of domestic policies.

Seen against the caution exercised in relation to international human rights law, Canada and other nations have delegated enormous authority to international trade tribunals. They have done so with little apparent consideration of the consequences for vital areas of domestic policy, including health, and without providing for a way to ensure consistency with their international human rights obligations.

International trade agreements, including the GATT/WTO agreements, NAFTA and the proposed FTAA, have been negotiated outside the purview of international political institutions. Through their ability to legally enforce their rulings, international trade tribunals now exercise a degree of authority which Canada and other national governments have been unwilling to delegate to the United Nations or to regional political organizations such as the Organization of American States.

While they are formally bound by the fundamental principles of international law, it is notable that NAFTA and the agreement which created the WTO include no explicit reference to the fundamental character of the Charter of the United Nations. Similarly, there are no provisions in the GATS nor in the WTO agreement governing the settlement of disputes to ensure that trade rules are interpreted consistently with international human rights obligations.

At the same time, the scope of recent international trade agreements has broadened so that almost no area of domestic policy is immune to a trade challenge. Trade liberalization is commonly understood to be about reducing tariffs and other "at-the-border" impediments to the flow of goods (and, more recently, services) across national borders. Since the Uruguay Round, however, international trade negotiations have increasingly focused on reducing so-called "non-tariff barriers" to trade, which potentially include any government measure which has the effect of limiting access by foreign producers and providers to its national market, or limiting their competitive opportunities once they are established in the country.

The NAFTA was a ground-breaking trade agreement when it was concluded in 1992. By including chapters on investment, services and intellectual property, it extended trade obligations into areas of national policy and regulation previously considered beyond the reach of trade ne-

Table 2: When Trade Rules Trump Health

NAFTA Cases

Tobacco
In 1994, the federal government let its plain packaging legislation die after representatives of Phillip Morris International and R.J. Reynolds Tobacco International argued that it constituted an expropriation of assets, violating the NAFTA investment and intellectual property obligations.[1] Although the tobacco companies did not launch a formal trade challenge, their threat – which was issued by lawyers who had held the most senior trade positions in the George Bush Sr. administration – clearly influenced the Canadian government's decision not to proceed with plain packaging legislation.

MMT (a gasoline additive)
In settlement of a NAFTA challenge by Ethyl Corporation, the federal government repealed a ban on the gasoline additive MMT. A major ingredient of MMT is manganese, a heavy metal known to cause brain damage in high doses. Ethyl Corporation was also paid US$13 million in compensation after it argued, on the strength of the NAFTA investment chapter, that the ban had the effect of expropriating its assets even if there was no "taking" in the classic understanding of expropriation.[2]

PCBs
Canada recently lost a dispute initiated by S.D. Meyers Inc, a hazardous waste disposal company, which claimed US$30 million for losses it allegedly incurred as a result of a Canadian ban on exports of PCBs in the mid-1990s. The NAFTA dispute panel decided in favour of the company, even though allowing PCB exports would have brought Canada into conflict with its commitments in the Basel Convention on the Transboundary Movement of Hazardous Wastes and with U.S. legislation banning PCB imports. A coalition of Canadian NGOs is urging the federal government to appeal this ruling.

MTBE (another gasoline additive)
A Canadian-based company, Methanex Corp., is suing the U.S. government for US$970 million in losses due to a California state order to phase out the use of MTBE, a methanol-based gasoline additive which has contaminated groundwater from leaks in underground storage tanks. The state governor has called MTBE "a significant risk to California's environment."

WTO Cases

Beef Hormones

In 1996 Canada and the United States challenged a European Union directive which banned imports of beef from livestock which had been fed certain growth-enhancing hormones. In 1998 the WTO Appellate Body upheld an earlier Dispute Panel decision which found that the EU ban did not meet the stringent risk assessment requirements of the WTO Agreement on Sanitary and Phytosanitary Measures. It also dismissed the EU argument that a ban on hormone-treated beef was justified by the precautionary principle. After the EU refused to withdraw its ban, the WTO permitted the U.S. and Canada to retaliate by raising tarrifs on EU products, at an annual cost to EU countries of US$130 million in lost exports.

Patent Protection for Drugs

The U.S. challenged Canada's system of compulsory licensing, arguing that prior to 1989 patent protection for pharmaceutical drugs was inconsistent with Canada's obligations under the Agreement on Trade-Related Intellectual Property Rights (TRIPS). In September 2000 the WTO Appellate Body upheld an earlier panel ruling, which required Canada to increase the protection for patents granted before 1989, when the Patent Act was amended to protect patents for 20 years from the date of filing a patent application. Generic drug manufacturers warned that extending the term for these patents could cost Canadian consumers as much as $200 million in higher drug prices. Canada has not yet indicated whether it will extend protection for the patents in question, or face trade retaliation.

Asbestos

In September 2000 Canada lost its GATT challenge of a French ban on imports of asbestos products. It was the first time in 53 years of dispute resolution at the GATT/WTO that a public health measure was successfully shielded from a trade challenge on public health grounds.

While the asbestos ruling was welcomed by health and environmental organizations, it is too early to tell whether it will help to shield other public health measures from trade challenges. Certain aspects of the decision — including the trade panel's decision to conduct its own assessment of public health risks, rather than defer to public health experts — are potentially damaging to future cases. The Government of Canada appears determined to pursue this trade challenge in defiance of environmental, public health and other concerns. Soon after the release of the WTO panel report, International Trade Minister Pierre Pettigrew announced that he will ask the WTO Appellate Body to overturn the panel decision.[1]

---

[1] DFAIT press release: "Canada to Appeal WTO Ruling in France Asbestos Dispute, 18 September 2000.

gotiators. In many respects, these NAFTA provisions influenced the Uruguay Round negotiations, which concluded in 1994 with, among other outcomes, the GATS framework agreement and the establishment of the World Trade Organization.[10]

Canada's investment obligations under NAFTA Chapter 11 have forced the federal government to repeal two significant public health measures – plain packaging for cigarettes, and a ban on the gasoline additive, MMT (which contains the human neurotoxin, manganese). Both cases illustrate how far "behind-the-border" Canada's NAFTA obligations already extend.

At the same time, Canada has shown no hesitation in using trade rules to challenge the health measures of other nations. It has pursued an aggressive trade policy, challenging the regulatory regimes of other nations on behalf of Canadian commercial interests (see summaries of EU beef hormone and Asbestos cases in Table 2). These actions arguably conflict with Canada's obligation under the Covenant to "respect the enjoyment of the right to health in other countries." Canada's aggressive pursuit of market access has influenced our position in WTO negotiations, where Canada has generally supported an ambitious agenda to further extend the reach of international trade and investment obligations.

WTO representatives and other trade officials often use the metaphor of a bicycle – which needs to keep moving forward in order to stay upright — to explain the ever-expanding scope of multilateral trade negotiations. Other commentators, including the OECD, have remarked more substantively on the implications of this trajectory:

"The progressive dismantling or lowering of traditional barriers to trade and increased relevance of 'behind the border' measures to effective market access and presence has exposed national regulatory regimes to a degree of unprecedented international scrutiny by trade and investment partners, with the result that regulation is no longer, if ever it was, a purely 'domestic' affair."[11]

Through its role in the GATS, Canada is playing a leading role in extending the reach of international trade rules ever deeper into areas of domestic policy.

General Agreement on Trade in Services (GATS)

While the WTO agenda is being pursued in numerous fora, Canada is particularly influential at the GATS negotiations which are chaired by Sergio Marchi, Canada's ambassador to the WTO and a former Minister of International Trade. These negotiations are part of the WTO's "built-in agenda." Their aim is to increase GATS coverage and extend its reach in a number of new directions.

The GATS framework agreement, which was concluded in 1994, is a complex agreement which breaks new ground in a number of areas. It established the following "architecture":

- general rules (such as most-favoured-nation status and commitments to transparency) which apply to all services;
- specific commitments to market access and national treatment which apply only to those services listed by countries in their schedules to the agreement;

- sectoral annexes that set out rules for particular sectors such as telecommunications and financial services; and
- an overarching commitment to "progressive liberalization" through successive rounds of negotiations to increase coverage and expand the GATS.

Each of these components, and their interaction, must be considered to adequately assess the implications of the agreement. Thus it is inaccurate to describe the GATS as simply a "bottom up" agreement which only affects those services that a country has positively listed in its schedule of specific commitments. There are important "top-down" features of the GATS which must also be considered. Those that have important implications for Canadian health services include the following:

- The GATS applies to any government measure "affecting trade in services." All measures are, in principle, covered by the GATS including laws, regulations, licensing standards and qualifications, guidelines and limitations on market access. If it affects "trade in services" (even incidentally or potentially), a measure introduced to achieve a health purpose is in principle covered by the GATS obligations.

- "Trade in services" is defined very expansively to include not just cross-border trade but every possible means of supplying a service including through electronic commerce, international travel and foreign investment. Furthermore, rulings in the first GATS disputes have established the principle that government measures cannot distinguish between different modes of supplying a service. This principle of "modal neutrality" could have far-reaching implications for the provision of health services, especially given the projected growth of telehealth applications.

- The GATS applies to measures taken by any level of government — including provincial and local governments and regional authorities – and to measures taken by non-governmental authorities exercising powers delegated by any level of government. Regional health authorities, regulatory bodies and not-for-profit health service providers are therefore covered by the GATS obligations.

- The GATS applies to most public services. Only services which meet a very narrow definition of services "provided in the exercise of governmental authority" are entirely excluded from the GATS obligations. Any service, including health care, which involves a mix of private and public funding and delivery appears to be subject to GATS obligations on the same basis as commercial services.

- The GATS covers all service sectors. The general rules, including MFN and transparency commitments, apply to all service sectors (other than those specifically exempted by individual countries). Without exception, all service sectors, including health, are on the table in the WTO GATS 2000 negotiations and subsequent rounds of negotiations.

The WTO GATS 2000 negotiations, which were launched in February 2000, will augment the GATS framework agreement on a number of fronts. These can be grouped into three sets of related negotiations, each of which may extend GATS coverage of health services:

- Rule making: This phase concerns the process and parameters of subsequent negotiations. The classification of services is a major focus, and how various health services are classified will determine whether they are covered by certain GATS obligations. Some governments are also supporting an effort to introduce new "horizontal negotiating modalities," which are intended to expand GATS coverage by employing additional cross-cutting rules or binding guidelines for negotiators. Such approaches could lead to extending coverage of health services, without requiring negotiators to make specific commitments that would draw political and public attention.

- Market access: A major aim of the WTO GATS 2000 negotiations is to increase member countries' specific commitments regarding services and measures subject to the market access and national treatment obligations. One approach may be to use "formula approaches" or other horizontal negotiating modalities to secure additional specific commitments. Another is to narrow the exclusions maintained by each country. Canada will inevitably face strong pressure from other countries to make commitments in health services, and to narrowly restrict the definition of any exclusions for health services.

- New obligations: The GATS framework agreement mandates negotiations on new obligations in a number of areas which further push the boundaries of international trade negotiations. These include domestic regulation, subsidies and government procurement. New GATS obligations in these areas could have far-reaching implications for the provision of health services.

While this study focuses on the implications of the GATS for Canada's health services, it is important to note that the GATS (and other trade agreements) may affect health in other ways.

1.4 Population Health: towards a framework for understanding the effect of trade liberalization

Health policy in Canada has a well-established tradition of innovation which addresses its commitments to fully realize the right to health, as set out in the International Covenant on Economic, Social and Cultural Rights. The population health approach, which Canadians have been instrumental in promoting, provides a good starting point for assessing the impact of trade liberalization on health.

A starting premise of the population health approach is that, more than the absence of disease, health is a resource for living. The Ottawa Charter for Health Promotion, endorsed by the Government of Canada and the WHO, defines health as follows:

> *Health is a state of complete physical, mental and social well-being and not merely the absence of disease or infirmity. It is the extent to which an*

> *individual or group is able, on the one hand, to*
> *realize aspirations and satisfy needs and, on the*
> *other hand, to change or cope with the environ-*
> *ment.*[12]

In this view health is determined by both individual and collective factors. A framework for understanding these factors, developed by the Federal, Provincial and Territorial Advisory Committee on Population Health (ACPH) in 1994,[13] has been widely adopted in Canada and elsewhere. Most recent versions of this framework[14] identify the following key determinants of health:

- Living and working conditions (socioeconomic environment)
- Physical environment

Figure 1: Framework for Population Health
(from Federal/Provincial/Territorial Advisory Council on Population Health, Strategies for Population Health, Health Canada: 1994)

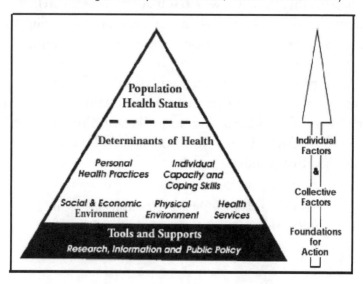

- Health services
- Early childhood development
- Social support
- Personal health practices and coping skills
- Biology and genetic endowment

These factors influence health, both directly and indirectly, and are themselves interconnected. While the contribution of each factor can be examined separately, "it is the interplay of all the factors that ultimately determines the health of individuals, families and communities."[15] As shown in Figure 1, the ACPH emphasizes that the more collective factors enable or provide the basis for the more individual factors determining health. It also emphasizes the importance of a wide range of public policies, and the need for intersectoral policy coordination to support population health. As the ACPH notes, this requires private business and economic policy makers to both understand how their decisions affect population health and act on that understanding:

> "It will be necessary to improve the understanding of other sectors about the ways in which their policies, decisions and actions impact population health. Furthermore, it will be necessary to bring about a willingness to act on that understanding, so their actions better support population health. A greater understanding in the economic and business sectors about the links between health and prosperity will be particularly crucial."[16]

Using the population health framework, a comprehensive study would require examining how trade policies affect health, not only through their impact on health services but also through impacts on other factors, including socioeconomic environment, physical environment, early child development, and social supports.

There is growing interest among health policy analysts in the impact of international trade. In an article published in a recent edition of the *Bulletin of the World Health Organization*, Yach, Bettcher and Guindon identify certain components of trade — health services, hazardous commodities and intellectual property — which influence health.[17] The authors identify specific ways in which these trade obligations affect health, both directly and indirectly. Ron Labonte et. al. have adapted this approach to propose four main "pathways" through which trade liberalization affects health: social and environmental health-determining conditions; regulatory pathways; trade in health-damaging products; and access to health-promoting services.[18]

Further research and policy work in this area can support collaboration among policy-makers in health, trade and other fields to ensure that interventions acting on the direct determinants of health are not hampered by conflicting trade obligations, and that appropriate policies are designed to address the indirect determinants of health.

The remainder of this book returns to the specific focus of our study on the implications of the GATS for Canada's health care system. The next chapter reviews the current state of our health care system, focusing on the financial and institutional arrangements which sustain it and on the policy challenges which face it. It also examines Canada's activities to promote the export of health services. Certain of these activities bring the federal government into conflict with the principles that underlie the Canadian health care system.

Chapter 2
Health Care in Canada, Market Access Abroad: Our Government's Conflicting Agendas

As I have stated before, public health and education are not on the table in any international trade negotiations. My government will maintain our right and ability to set and maintain the principles of our public health and education. It is that simple, and those who wish to pick away at issues, to find threats in every trade agreement to our values, our social system, are simply wrong.

–The Honourable Pierre Pettigrew, Minister of International Trade, statement to the Standing Committee on Foreign Affairs and International Trade, 14 June 2000 (Hansard, 1540).

The SAGIT is supportive of any opportunities for Canadians to increase their ability to offer their services internationally. Members cautioned that there would be a price to pay, i.e., granting similar opportunities to foreigners.

–Letter from Brian Harling, chair of the Medical and Health Care Products & Services SAGIT (Sectoral Advisory Group on International Trade) and Vice-President (Corporate Affairs and Government Relations) of

MDS Inc., to The Honourable Pierre
Pettigrew, Minister of International Trade, 21
March 2000.

Public opinion polls show that health care is consistently
the single issue about which Canadians are most concerned.
There is strong public support for Canada's health care
system but also equally strong public fear that the system
is in trouble and that Canadians can no longer count on
receiving medical attention when they need it.

In this climate of uncertainty the Government of Canada
has repeatedly reaffirmed its support for the values and
principles on which our health system are based. The Prime
Minister, the Health Minister and probably every member
of the government have publicly committed themselves to
upholding the five conditions of Medicare set out in the
Canada Health Act, namely: public administration, comprehensiveness, universality, portability and accessibility.

Government ministers have also assured Canadians that
our participation in trade agreements will not jeopardize
Canada's health care system. Pierre Pettigrew's recent statement to the Standing Committee on Foreign Affairs and
International Trade, quoted above, echoes many such assurances made by him and other members of the government.

Unfortunately, the reality is neither as simple nor as re-
assuring as Mr.Pettigrew asserts. As the next section of this
report shows, health care services are currently covered by
the general rules of the GATS framework agreement, and
certain health care services are also covered by Canada's
specific commitments. Moreover, there are strong grounds
to fear that the GATS 2000 negotiations, if unchallenged,

will extend GATS coverage to a wider range of health services, and establish disciplines which would further diminish Canadians' ability to regulate and change how health services are provided.

As important background to our analysis of the health implications of the GATS, this section first briefly reviews how health services are financed and delivered in Canada, then identifies some of the important public policy issues which Canadians and our governments now face regarding the future of health care in Canada.

Full knowledge of this context is beyond the capacity of any single group of trade negotiators, including Canada's delegation to the GATS negotiations. But without such knowledge, negotiators may very well be unaware of the health implications of positions they take in Geneva. And without an adequate appreciation of the values and principles that define our health system, nor the political direction to give them precedence over commercial objectives, Canadian negotiators may actively pursue objectives that undermine Canadian health care.

The second part of this section reviews the federal government strategy to expand international markets for Canadian health services exports. It argues that this strategy conflicts with the government's stated commitment to protecting Canada's health care system – a point of view reinforced by the industry representative quoted above. If allowed to influence Canada's negotiating position at the GATS negotiations, the commercial interests driving Canada's strategy for exporting health services could very well undermine the regulatory framework and institutions that sustain our health care system.

A Mixed System

> *Canada has a predominantly publicly financed, privately delivered health care system that is best described as an interlocking set of ten provincial and three territorial health insurance plans. Known to Canadians as "Medicare," the system provides access to universal, comprehensive coverage for medically necessary hospital, in-patient and out-patient physician services.*
>
> –Health Canada, "Canada's Health Care System," (pamphlet, July 1999) available on the web: www.hc-sc.gc.ca/datapcb/datahesa/E-sys.htm.

These two sentences neatly encapsulate a complex health system. Public health insurance funds Canadians' access to medically necessary services, most of which are provided privately by independent physicians and other professionals and by private not-for-profit hospitals and other facilities.

As a condition of delivering publicly funded services, these private providers are licensed and regulated by a number of bodies, including provincial governments and agencies, colleges of physicians and other regulatory bodies. Health regulations address a number of public purposes, including access and quality of services, ethical concerns and cost controls. In addition, provincial health insurance plans must comply with the principles of the Canada Health Act in order to be eligible for full federal transfers.

Figure 2: Schematic of Public and Private Financing of Canada's Health System

(from National Forum on Health, *The Public and Private Financing of Canada's Health System* (September 1995)

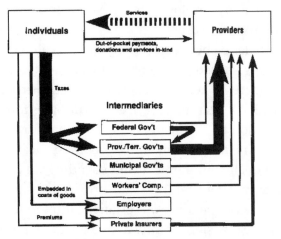

Figure 2 shows the various sources of funding for Canada's health services[1]. Total health spending amounted to $86 billion in 1999, of which $59.8 billion (69.6%) is public spending funded by tax revenue.[2]

Provincial and territorial governments, which receive large transfers from the federal government, are the largest direct funders — through health insurance, transfers to regional health authorities and hospitals, funding of community health clinics, purchase of services, and other spending. The federal government directly funds health services for First Nations and Inuit peoples, veterans and military personnel, as well as health protection and surveillance and health promotion services for the general population. Municipal governments also directly fund certain health services, including public health and health promotion services.

There are several sources of private spending on health, which amounted to $26.2 billion in 1999 (30.4% of total health spending). These include out-of-pocket payments by individuals, premiums paid to private insurers, and premiums paid by employers to workers' compensation plans and to private insurers.

The balance between public and private spending on health has shifted in recent years. As table 3 shows, the public share of health spending has fallen from the 75% level which it occupied for over two decades following the introduction of Medicare.[3] This was the result of federal and provincial government cost-cutting measures which led to a decline in public health spending (in constant per capita terms) between 1993 and 1996. At the same time per capita private spending on certain health services has continued to grow significantly above the rate of inflation.

Between 1990 and 1997, annual per capita private spending increased by 3.7% on drugs, 2.9% on health professionals other than physicians, 3.5% on health facilities other than hospitals, and 6.9% on the residual category of "other health expenditures."[4] The diversity of services covered by the latter three categories makes it difficult to pinpoint the causes of growth in private sector spending. There is evi-

Table 3: Private and Public Sector Expenditure
1960-1997

	Total ($ millions)	Private Sector ($ millions)	Percent Private	Private / GDP	Public Sector ($ millions)	Percent Public	Public / GDP
1960	2,142	1,226	57.3%	3.1%	915	42.7%	2.3%
1965	3,415	1,636	47.9%	2.9%	1,779	52.1%	3.1%
1970	6,254	1,864	29.8%	2.1%	4,389	70.2%	5.0%
1975	12,260	2,899	23.6%	1.7%	9,361	76.4%	5.4%
1980	22,353	5,457	24.4%	1.7%	16,897	75.6%	5.4%
1985	39,889	9,747	24.4%	2.0%	30,143	75.6%	6.2%
1990	61,229	15,571	25.4%	2.3%	45,658	74.6%	6.7%
1997	77,077	23,312	30.2%	2.7%	53,765	69.8%	6.3%

dence, however, that it is being driven in part by an unprecedented increase in private for-profit hospitals and clinics. Some of these operate purely privately, charging wealthy clients the full fee for their services. But a number also provide services under contract to provincial ministries of health, raising public policy issues about the extent to which public health budgets fund the profits of commercial health providers.[5]

A diverse web of financial and administrative arrangements underlie this aggregate picture. Table 4, adapted from a study prepared for the National Forum on Health, summarizes how particular health services are financed and delivered.[6] [7]

These diverse arrangements involving the federal government plus 13 provincial and territorial jurisdictions are knit together into a national health system by common principles which are expressed in conditions on public funding, licensing, and other forms of regulation.

The highest legal expression of principles related to health services is found in the Constitution Act of 1982, which affirms the principle of equalizaton payments "to ensure that provincial governments have sufficient revenues to provide reasonably comparable levels of public services at reasonably comparable levels of taxation."[8]

The Canada Health Act of 1984 established more specific principles regarding the provision of health services. Because the delivery of health services is within provincial/territorial jurisdiction (other than the exceptions noted above), the federal government role is exercised through its spending power. Accordingly, the CHA principles are expressed as "program criteria" which provincial health insurance plans must satisfy in order to qualify for full federal cash transfers.

Table 4
Financing and Delivery of Canadian Health Services

Service Type	Financing (1999 spending figures)	Delivery
Hospital services	Total spending $27.2 billion, 90.2% of which is public spending. 100% public for medically necessary services (no user charges permitted); private payment for upgraded accommodation or non-medically necessary services provided in hospitals.	Mixed public/private. Varies across provinces. Government generally exerts a strong influence.
Physician Services	Total spending: $12 billion; of which 98.8% is public spending. 100% public for medically necessary services (no extra billing permitted); private payment for non-medically necessary services.	Private – physicians are independent and self-regulating; some models of primary care delivery (e.g. CLSCs in Quebec) are more akin to government agencies.
Services provided in private for-profit clinics	Services not defined as medically necessary are fully privately funded. Some clinics provide medically necessary services, and charge a facility fee over and above funding from provincial health insurance plans. Alberta Bill 11 permits private for-profit clinics to provide certain hospital services, and charge additional fees in addition to publicly insured amounts.	Privately owned and operated – limited regulation.
Dental/optometry care	Mostly private spending (insurance and out-of-pocket); some provincial plans provide coverage for children and seniors. (51% of Canadians reported private health insurance coverage for glasses or contact lenses, and slightly more reported coverage for dental care. (1998/99 National Population Health Survey, reported in CIHI, Health Care in Canada, p.20).	Private and self-regulating.
Prescription drugs	Total spending: $13.1 billion, of which 32.2% is public spending (incl non-prescription drugs and personal health supplies). Full public payment for prescription drugs dispensed in hospitals. Provincial plans pay for approximately 40% of all prescription drugs dispensed outside hospitals. Coverage is typically limited to seniors, welfare recipients and cases of catastrophic illness (e.g. AIDS, Hepatitis C). Balance is funded by a combination of private insurance plans and out-of-pocket payments.	Private – delivery includes prescription by physician and dispensing by pharmacist or hospital.

Non-prescription drugs	Mostly private out-of-pocket payment.	Private – over –the-counter
Services of other professionals (incl. mid-wives, psychologists, physiotherapists, chiropractors, private duty nurses)	Total spending: $11 billion, of which 9.8% is public spending. Mostly private insurance and out-of-pocket payment. Provincial health insurance in Ontario and B.C. have recently been extended to cover midwifery services.	Private (e.g. physiologists, physiotherapists, chiropractors, midwives, private duty nurses)
Alternative/Complementary medicines (incl. traditional Aboriginal healers, naturopaths, homeopaths, practitioners of oriental medicine)	Mostly private insurance and out-of-pocket payments. Some limited coverage by certain provincial plans, e.g. oriental medicine in B.C., services of traditional Aboriginal healers in Ontario.	Private – e.g. naturopaths, homeopaths, practitioners of oriental medicine, traditional Aboriginal healers.
Long-term care (residential)	Mixed public/private: public portion covers insured health care services, private portion covers room and board.	Mixed public/private. There has been a rapid increase in private for-profit nursing homes, which often provide care to persons who are seriously ill or infirm.
Home care *may overlap with "services of other professionals"	Total spending estimated at $3.4 billon, of which 79.4% is estimated to be public spending. Partial public coverage in most jurisdictions. No definitive data is available, in part because of the difficulties of accounting for uncompensated care by family members, and distinguishing between spending on health and spending on household consumption; a 1998 Health Canada report estimates that public spending on home care was $2.1 billion in 1997-98.	Mixed public/private. Public delivery in Manitoba.
Ambulance services	Partial public coverage in some provinces; special programs for residents of remote areas.	Mostly private operators.
Public health programs	Public	Public, mostly federal and local government
Services to First Nations and Inuit	Public	Mixed public/private. In many areas, services provided directly by the federal government are being transferred to First Nations and Inuit governments.

Sources: this table adapts and updates a table prepared for the National Forum on Health, "The Public and Private Financing of Canada's Health System, September 1996, p.6. All 1999 spending figures are from the Canadian Institute for Health Information, *Health Care in Canada: a first annual report (2000)*, except home care estimate which is from Peter Coyte, "Home Care in Canada: Passing the Buck" University of Toronto, May 2000
© CCPA

The Canada Health Act defines the principles of Medicare as follows:

- Public Administration: *the health care insurance plan of a province must be administered and operated on a non-profit basis by a public authority appointed or designated by the government of the province;*

- Comprehensiveness: *the health care insurance plan of a province must insure all insured health services provided by hospitals, medical practitioners or dentists, and where the law of the province so permits, similar or additional services rendered by other health care practitioners;*

- Universality: *the health care insurance plan of a province must entitle one hundred per cent of the insured persons of the province to the insured health services provided for by the plan on uniform terms and conditions;*

- Portability: *the health care insurance plan of a province (a) must not impose any minimum period of residence in the province, or waiting period, in excess of three months before residents of the province are eligible for or entitled to insured health services;* and *(b) must provide for the payment of amounts for the cost of insured health services provided to insured persons while temporarily absent from the province;*

- Accessibility: *the health care insurance plan of a province must provide for insured health services on uniform terms and conditions and on a basis that does not impede or preclude, either directly or indirectly, whether by charges made to insured persons or otherwise, reasonable access to those services by insured persons.*

Because most health services are delivered at the provincial level, these principles are effective only to the extent they are reflected in provincial measures which affect how insured health services are provided. These measures include provincial health insurance legislation; regulations specifying insured services; licensing of physicians, nurses and other health professionals; billing numbers; fee schedules for insured services; physicians; and hospital charters.

New challenges in health care require governments to constantly review these measures and adjust how services are delivered. Canada's ability to develop a common approach to renewing Medicare is complicated by the different circumstances and diverging interests of the various federal and provincial governments. This difficulty, which is inherent to federalism, has created opportunities for commercial health care providers.

Health Care at the Crossroads

Public policy debate about the future of health care now centres on Canada's capacity to uphold the five principles of Medicare on a financially sustainable basis.

Cuts in public spending during the 1990s were coupled with cost pressures driven by changes in demography and disease patterns, the development of costly new technologies and treatments, an increasing reliance on high-cost drug therapies, and other factors. [9] Government measures to manage these pressures – which include de-listing insured services, reducing staff and beds in hospitals and long term care facilities, and contracting out food, laundry and other support services — have in some cases compromised Canadians' access to medical services.

While support for the Canadian health care system remains very strong, many Canadians fear that medical treatment will not be available to them when they need it. This fear is reinforced by the public and media attention given to cases of overflowing emergency rooms, bed shortages, and long waiting periods for specialist procedures.

Initiatives to expand the provision of community-based services have not progressed rapidly enough to offset the effect of cuts to hospitals and other institutional facilities. And, with no national direction on how best to reform the delivery of primary health services in order to optimize the use of health resources, provincial and territorial governments have pursued divergent approaches. In some cases, most notably Alberta and Ontario, these approaches include increasing the commercial provision of health services.

Alberta's legislation to allow public financing of insured services provided by commercial for-profit hospitals strikes at the heart of the Canadian health system. If such facilities are established, with their fees paid partially by provincial health insurance, they directly challenge the principles of universality and accessibility. In exchange for an additional private fee, these facilities offer access to insured services more rapidly, or with better perceived quality, thereby violating the universality requirement that all insured citizens be entitled to insured services "on uniform terms and conditions." And because they would inevitably exclude those unable to pay the private fee, these facilities would violate the accessibility principle.

These events challenge provincial and territorial governments to address vital public policy issues. Are we re-

signed to having a two-tier health system in which commercial facilities provide preferential access for Canadians
able to afford additional out-of-pocket fees? Is Medicare
sustainable only with a more restrictive definition of "medically necessary services"? Or can the delivery of health services be reorganized to more cost-effectively provide access
to a broader range of insured services, including homecare
and prescription drugs? How can rising drug costs be contained? What can governments do to keep Canadians more
healthy by better addressing the determinants of health?

Recent increases in federal health transfers have not reduced the urgency of these and other issues. In their recent
Health Accord, the First Ministers outlined the following
priorities for collaboration among governments.[10]

1) Access to care
2) Health promotion and wellness
3) Appropriate health care services – primary health care
4) Supply of doctors, nurses and other health personnel
5) Home care and community care
6) Pharmaceuticals management
7) Health information and communications technology
8) Health equipment and infrastructure

There are diverging views within Canada on all these
issues. To give only one example, the journal of the Canadian Medical Association recently called for a review of
the Canada Health Act, specifically the definition of comprehensiveness which it characterizes as "broad and perhaps unaffordable".

> *The real worry is that with ever-increasing pri-*
> *vatization of health care ... the principles of the*

> *Act ... may not be sustainable. ... The bounda-*
> *ries of comprehensiveness are enlarging both be-*
> *cause of scientific advance and because expecta-*
> *tions about what is medically necessary – home*
> *care, chronic care, drugs and preventive care, for*
> *example – are increasing. ...It is time to re-ex-*
> *amine the principles of the Canada Health Act*
> *and to be more precise in our notions of compre-*
> *hensiveness and medical necessity.*[11]

Other commentators stress the need to stem the growth of commercial health services, in order to maintain and renew Medicare. Robert Evans, a preeminent health economist, observes that the extraordinary growth of for-profit health services cannot be reconciled with "the mutual adaptation and containment" required to sustain Medicare.[12] This view shifts attention towards changing the way services are provided within the public system instead of restricting Canadians' entitlement to those services.

For instance, former federal Health Minister Monique Bégin argues that a precise definition of "medical necessity" is not feasible and emphasis instead should be given to primary care reform, including changes to the roles of physicians and other health professionals and to how they are compensated. Such changes, she argues, could enable cost-effective coverage of the complete spectrum of health services, including home care, long-term care and mental health community care.[13]

Former Saskatchewan premier Roy Romanow has similarly emphasized the need for primary care reform, but suggests that some rationing of health services is required while advocating more attention to addressing the determinants of health.[14]

It is properly the responsibility of elected governments to address these and other issues regarding the future of Canada's health system. To act in the public interest, governments need the flexibility to adjust policies, regulations and other measures in response to changing circumstances.

Monique Bégin emphasizes the fluidity and fragility of our health system:

> *The health care system in Canada is the result of the constantly renegotiated and fragile equilibrium between three key partners: the provincial governments, the federal government, and organized medicine. None is over and above the others; none has the control of the system. Each can disrupt it seriously, yet all are needed to make it function smoothly.*[15]

An appreciation of the mutable character of our health system, and of how government legislation and regulations give effect to the principles of Medicare, obliges us to ensure that Canada does not enter into trade agreements which foreclose public policy options in favour of short-sighted commercial interests. Otherwise, the federal government will tie its own hands, and those of provincial and local governments, and cede to commercial health corporations more power in determining the future of Canada's health system.

Promoting health services exports: at what price?

While Canadians debate the future of Medicare and the federal government pledges to uphold the principles of the

Canada Health Act, Industry Canada and the Department of Foreign Affairs and International Trade (DFAIT) are working aggressively to expand international markets for Canadian health services exports. The approach adopted by the federal government, working closely with commercial health corporations, involves targeting as "barriers to market access" the foreign counterparts to many of the domestic regulations and policies which support the Canadian health care system.

The primary strategic documents defining the Government of Canada's export promotion priorities are the Canadian International Business Strategy reports (CIBS) developed by "Trade Team Canada" committees. These interdepartmental committees, which include senior industry representatives, aim to provide exporters with a single point of contact in government. Their work establishes priorities for the ongoing work of Canadian trade missions, as well as for the high-profile Team Canada missions led by the Prime Minister and other First Ministers.

The CIBS for health industries identifies telehealth services as its single priority for Canada's export promotion activities in the health services sector.[16] Industry Canada defines telehealth services very broadly to encompass "the use of communications and information technology to deliver health and health care services and information over large and small distances."

Thus telehealth is not a distinct service, but a medium which has many applications across the entire range of health services. The CIBS sub-divides telehealth into the following categories:

- Diagnostic and patient care: the remote provision of clinical services to an individual either at home or at a clinical site;

- Peacekeeping, battlefield and victim assistance services: the remote provision of clinical services to military personnel and disaster victims;
- Professional backup: the remote support to health care providers from providers with specialized expertise;
- Consumer health information: the online delivery of health related information for decision-making and self-service by consumers;
- Continuing professional education: the distance delivery of continuing professional education to health providers; and
- Management of health delivery systems: the remote provision of administrative services in support of health care delivery.

These applications promise many benefits for health services in Canada and other countries. Enabling physicians to consult patients by video-conferencing, and physicians to exchange x-rays and other medical images with specialists can provide remote or isolated communities with quick and affordable access to health services. Online connections to drug information databases can supply physicians and pharmacists with the most up-to-date information on drug interactions, and facilitate cost-containment through the use of drug formularies. Twenty-four-hour telephone advice lines – a service provided by a number of Canadian hospitals – connect families with a nurse and can avoid unnecessary emergency room visits for common ailments. Integrating hospital administrative services into regional networks can facilitate the use of current health information to allocate resources and to develop policy.

However, introducing telehealth applications in Canada and elsewhere raises numerous ethical, legal and regulatory issues with significant implications for health care policy. Permitting physicians to be compensated for remote consultations would require changes to provincial health insurance plans, including new methods of monitoring for fraudulent billings. The ability of a physician based in one jurisdiction to provide services to a patient in another jurisdiction raises questions for licensing bodies, and for provincial policies regulating the number of practitioners with billing privileges.

Transmitting patient records electronically raises privacy and confidentiality concerns. The legal liability of physicians is also a question: how could criminal charges and insurance claims be pursued when a physician is licensed in a jurisdiction other than the one in which a case of malpractice occurred?

These are important public policy issues which are only just starting to be addressed in Canada, despite an enormous public investment in building the infrastructure for telehealth services (known as Canada's Health Info-way). As discussed in the next section of this report, our ability to ensure that telehealth applications support the principles of Medicare may be impaired by GATS obligations which restrict the ability of governments to differentiate between service providers on the basis of how a service is delivered or where the provider is based. In other countries, as in Canada, these difficult public policy issues should be addressed through democratically accountable public processes, not determined by trade panels. [17]

Regardless of these complications, the CIBS outlines an aggressive strategy to support Canadian companies in gaining access to telehealth markets in other countries. Based on private sector forecasts, the CIBS predicts enormous growth in global demand for commercial telehealth services. It makes the extraordinary claim that "Global demand for direct patient care telehealth services by the year 2000 is estimated to be at least US$800 *billion* (emphasis added)." This figure is hardly credible, given, for example, that the WTO estimates total commercial services trade in every sector amounted to US$1.3 trillion in 1998.[18] Conceptual and practical difficulties make it very difficult to accurately record the value of trade in services, let alone forecast into the future.[19]

Home care is emphasized as a key area of growing demand for commercial telehealth services, particularly in the U.S. and Japan where there is a growing elderly population that is wealthy and computer-literate. The CIBS notes that the "U.S. homecare market is estimated at US$16 billion and is the most rapidly growing segment of that health care market."[20] A DFAIT market report for New England estimates that 20% of home care visits could be replaced by telehealth services, including remote assessments and monitoring.[21]

Other key growth areas include commercial telehealth applications in administrative support and management of health information, direct provision of consumer health information, and continuing professional education.

The CIBS sets out a strategy for securing a significant share of these markets by, among other things, targeting the regulatory measures maintained by other countries. It notes that many non-tariff barriers exist despite the implementation of NAFTA and WTO agreements:

> *Factors that impact on market access include patent policy, regulatory review processes, Mutual Recognition Agreements (MRAs), and the use of "managed care" instruments such as for-*

mularies, procurement and utilization policies by health care managers in the public and private sectors.[22]

With specific reference to telehealth exports, the CIBS identifies the following "barriers to market entry":

- *Mutual recognition of professional credentials: while mutual recognition is being addressed at GATS, there is usually still a need to requalify in each jurisdiction in which a health care professional wishes to provide direct patient services.*
- *Malpractice insurance coverage of out-of-jurisdiction medical personnel: the ability to enforce revocation in the case of malpractice or negligence is dependent on linking practice in external jurisdictions to retention of licensure in one's home jurisdiction.*
- *Remuneration of health providers for remote consultations: in many jurisdictions face-to-face consultations are required to reduce the potential for fraudulent billings. Norway has recently had legislative success in implementing a fee schedule for telehealth services, which can serve as a model.*
- *Remuneration of health care providers from outside the jurisdiction: since health care and health insurance regimes are typically regulated at the sub-federal level, there is often no provision to "cover" services from professionals who do not reside in that jurisdiction.*
- *Patient privacy and confidentiality concerns: since telehealth can require a range of electronic transmissions of patient information, concerns about the security of data will have to be addressed by building infrastructure for the security of health networks that meets international standards.*[23]

These measures concern regulatory issues of crucial importance to the viability of any country's health system: maintaining professional standards and qualifications; guarding against malpractice and fraud; containing costs; and ensuring patient privacy and confidentiality. To identify them as "barriers to market access" for Canadian telehealth exports is to target in other countries the counterparts to the regulatory regimes which support the Canadian health system.

In addition to being inconsistent with our domestic policy commitments, Canada's export promotion policy may bring it into conflict with our obligations under the International Covenant on Economic, Social and Cultural Rights.

As previously noted, Canada's obligation to realize the right to health extends to its international relations. It is arguable that targeting the health policies of other countries is inconsistent with the obligation "to respect the enjoyment of the right to health in other countries." Furthermore, Canada's willingness to use its negotiating leverage in pursuit of the commercial objectives of health services exporters appears to contradict the obligation to prevent private businesses and other "third parties" from violating the right to health in other countries.

DFAIT officials maintain that CIBS priorities do not directly influence Canada's GATS negotiating position.[24] Canada's health services exporters, including those involved in developing the CIBS, however, receive privileged access in preparing the Government of Canada's negotiating position. The SAGIT for Medical and Healthcare Products and Services is chaired by a vice-president of MDS Inc., a company which led the commercialization of diagnostic health services in Canada and blossomed into "Canada's largest and most aggressive health and life-sciences corporation."[25] The SAGIT provides representatives of Canada's other major commercial health corporations with direct access to the Minister for International Trade, and a venue for continually raising concerns about trade policy.

Canadian health corporations also have access to highly effective international channels for influencing the outcome of the GATS negotiations. Private sector intervention at the GATS has been led by the U.S.-based Coalition of Service Industries, which has been widely credited with playing a key role in shaping the GATS framework agreement. David Hartridge, Director of the WTO Services Division, even credits major corporate members of the CSI with a critical role in salvaging the Uruguay Round and creating the GATS and the WTO.[26]

As part of its preparations for the GATS 2000 negotiations, the CSI is a key sponsor of the annual International Summit on the Private Health Sector, a gathering of senior health care managers from the public and private sectors. The objectives of the summit are as follows:

- Monitor regional and national health reforms important to the profitability and practices of the private sector;
- Promote the globalization of health care services and trade;
- Encourage direct dialogue among senior executives from the public and private health sectors;
- Address the troublesome, time-consuming management challenges confronting both public and private healthcare executives;
- Foster health alliances and business partnerships across national borders;

- Assist international companies, global agencies and healthcare thought leaders to publicize their mission statements, policy directions and health improvement projects;
- Gather competitive market information for health investors;
- Develop stronger public interest frameworks for the private health sector;
- Advance a shared commitment to health justice. [27]

Appropriate to its timing just prior to the next stage of GATS 2000 negotiations, the December 2000 summit included an executive seminar titled "World Trade Organization and International Trade in Health Services."

As the chair of the SAGIT makes clear in a letter to the Minister, Canadian health services exporters have no illusions that gaining market access to other countries will not require trade-offs to open the Canadian health system to commercial competition:

> *The SAGIT is supportive of any opportunities for Canadians to increase their ability to offer their services internationally. Members cautioned that there would be a price to pay, i.e., granting similar opportunities to foreigners.*[28]

Companies like MDS have grown in Canada by encouraging the incremental commercialization of health services. They stand to benefit from the much more dramatic privatization that could result from extending GATS coverage to insured health services, including hospital care, and to emerging high growth sectors such as home care. Extending market access to foreign companies would be a small price to pay for gaining access to these potentially lucrative public health budgets. Indeed, these companies benefit by increased commercialization both at home and abroad.

In fact, commercialization of Canadian health care is considered a condition for enhancing the capacity of Canadian firms to compete internationally. A sector competitiveness report prepared by Industry Canada in 1998 includes an analysis of how health care reform has promoted the growth of a commercial telehealth industry. The health reform items seen as contributing to the growth of a competitive telehealth industry include: reduced public funding, increased revenue generation, and increases in privately funded services.[29]

In assessing the capacity of Canadian companies to compete internationally, the CIBS notes that "In Canada, there is a strong desire to maintain universal access to publicly funded health care, while private sector sourcing of health services is growing under the imperatives of cost driven health reforms." "*Provided domestic barriers to growth are addressed,*" it goes on to conclude, "Canada has the potential to capture 10% of key world telehealth markets by the year 2005."[30] Behind the even-handed phrases there is a strong inference that further deregulation and commercialization at home are needed to expand Canadian export markets abroad.

The emphasis these companies, supported by the Government of Canada, have given to securing greater market access for telehealth services requires particular caution. Because telehealth services cut across the entire spectrum of health care services, any liberalizing measures to secure market access will have very broad consequences. And, as discussed in the next section of this report, recent WTO panel rulings, which give a very forceful interpretation of what constitute "like" services and service providers, give commercial health corporations added leverage to use telehealth services in securing greater access to public health spending.

Instead of acting as cheerleader for the global ambitions of commercial health service companies – to the point of repeating specious forecasts for market growth – the Government of Canada should very carefully consider the implications of its export promotion strategy for the integrity of Canada's health system.

Sadly, Canada's recent record indicates it will make aggressive use of NAFTA and WTO obligations to advance commercial interests, with little consideration of domestic policy implications and regardless of their health and environmental implications. In the EC beef hormone ban and the asbestos cases (summarized in Table 2), the federal government has challenged important public health measures of other jurisdictions on behalf of Canadian commercial interests of minor economic significance.

Commenting on the government's decision to appeal the recent WTO asbestos ruling, M.P. Bill Blaikie spells out the implications of this aggressive trade posture for domestic policy and politics:

> "Often, while a given nation is fighting a WTO ruling against a national policy of its own, it is simultaneously trying to use the WTO to strike down a national policy of another government which is harmful to the interests of its exporters. In these various challenges, each nation may win occasional victories for its exporters, but it loses many more cases on behalf of its broader citizenry.

The outcome is a radically diminished scope for democracy in all nations."[31]

Without a significant change in Canada's orientation at the WTO, there is good reason to believe that Canada will soon be involved in new trade disputes over alleged "barriers to market access" for health services. The economic clout of Canadian and transnational health services corporations far exceeds that of the commercial interests Canada has represented in recent WTO and NAFTA disputes. They are organizing internationally to ensure that the GATS 2000 negotiations extend GATS coverage of health services.

Commercial health services corporations find a receptive partner in the Government of Canada, which appears intent on pursuing its leadership role at the GATS with a reckless commitment to expanding the coverage of GATS disciplines and further restricting "behind-the-border" regulatory measures. Despite its reassurances that Canada's health system will not be affected, the federal government has not conducted a systematic analysis of the health implications of our existing GATS commitments. Whether future trade disputes involve the federal government as defendant of our health care regulations and institutions, or as challenger of those of other nations, Canadian citizens will be the losers.

Chapter 3
Overview of GATS Implications for Health Care

...there are certain domestic services sectors in which our interest in undertaking further liberalization may be limited. The Canadian government intends to continue to uphold its clearly defined and long-established objectives to safeguard Canada's freedom of action in key service sectors, including health, education and culture.

—DFAIT, Opening Doors to the World: Canada's international market access priorities 2000, 5 April 2000

As discussed before, trade in medical, health and social services is strongly influenced by measures not normally considered to be "trade measures." These may include (i) licensing and qualification requirements designed to ascertain the quality of the services provided and the integrity of professionals; (ii) restrictions on the range of goods and services professionals and hospitals are allowed to provide; (iii) controls or incentives intended to ensure the adequate provision of services in all regions and for all population groups; and (iv) the direct provision, on social policy grounds, of minimum services to economically disadvantaged groups.

Despite their restrictive or discriminatory (side-)effects, views may differ among Members whether these measures would need to be scheduled in all cases.

—WTO Council for Trade in Services, *Health and Social Services: background note by the Secretariat*, S/C/W/50 (18 September 1998), paragraphs 61 and 62.

The perspective of the WTO Secretariat quoted above jars with the more common view of health policy measures. In most public policy discourse any effect a government health measure might have on commercial services is regarded as incidental to the primary policy objective of the measure – i.e., preventing and treating disease, illness and injury; and maintaining and promoting health. If discriminatory effects are considered at all, the appropriate public policy question is whether any adjustments can be made to the measure without impairing its underlying public purpose, not whether it should be subordinated to international trade rules "in all cases."

Whether or not Canada includes health services in its GATS schedule of specific commitments, however, is only part of the story. Certain GATS rules apply to all services, whether or not they are scheduled. Components of Canada's health system are classified in categories of services which are already covered by Canada's specific GATS commitments. And the GATS 2000 negotiations, in which all services are on the table, are likely to extend GATS coverage of health services by increasing Canada's specific commitments and by other means.

This overview chapter examines first how the current GATS framework agreements applies to health services, then how the GATS 2000 negotiations might extend GATS coverage of health services.[1] Implications for specific health services are discussed in the following chapter.

GATS Framework Agreement: How are Canadian health services now covered?

To assess coverage of health services in the GATS framework agreement it is necessary to examine the general rules which apply to all services, the rules which apply only where Canada has made specific commitments, and how health services are classified in the GATS.

General rules

As previously mentioned, the GATS applies, in principle, to all services and to any government measure affecting trade in services. And, because "trade in services" is defined expansively, the scope of the GATS is even greater than first appears. It applies to any government measure that might affect competitive conditions relating to the supply of a service.

Modes of supply

Article I of the GATS defines trade in services as comprising four distinct "modes of supply": cross-border, consumption abroad, commercial presence, and presence of natural persons. This definition extends far beyond conventional notions of international trade, and covers every possible means by which a firm or individual based in one country could provide a service to individuals in another country. While cross-border supply resembles the conventional notion of a service crossing international borders (including by electronic means), the other modes include foreign investment (commercial presence) and international travel by individual service consumers (consumption abroad) or individual providers (presence of natural persons).

In its primer on the GATS, the WTO Secretariat is clear about the implications of this wide definition:

> The reach of the GATS rules extend to all forms of international trade in services. This means that the GATS represents a major new factor for a large sector of world economic activity. It also means, because such a large share of trade in services takes place **inside** national economies, that its requirements will from the beginning necessarily influence national domestic laws and regulations in a way that has been true of the GATT only in recent years. *(emphasis in the original)*[2]

Because it applies to an almost unlimited range of "behind-the-border" measures, the potential for the GATS to affect the provision of health services is far greater than would be expected of a conventional trade agreement. The GATS definition of a "measure" includes any "law, regulation, rule, procedure, decision, administrative action, or any other form" of measure.[3] In its background note on health and social services, the WTO Secretariat is equally candid on this matter:

There is hardly any measure governing the organization of the sector or the provision of individual services that would not affect, directly or indirectly, access conditions under one of the four modes covered by GATS.[4]

Exclusions and exceptions

The GATS includes a few provisions to exclude or except certain government measures from its general obligations. These are narrowly defined and are unlikely to shield much of Canada's health system.

Article 1:3 excludes "services supplied in the exercise of governmental authority" from the scope of the Agreement. It further specifies that this phrase "means any service which is supplied neither on a commercial basis nor in competition with one or more service suppliers." This narrow definition may cover such services as central banking and statutory social security. But, because the Canadian health system comprises a combination of financing sources — both public and private — and a mix of predominantly private service providers, most health services are unlikely to meet the conditions of this exclusion.

Article XIV(b) preserves the ability of Member governments to adopt or enforce measures "necessary to protect human, animal or plant life or health." Based on GATT and WTO jurisprudence, this exception will provide very limited protection for health measures. Dispute panels have established a very stringent "necessity test" for measures to be shielded by the condition of the identically worded general exception in the GATT (article XXb). Until the recent Asbestos decision, in over 50 years of jurisprudence, no GATT or WTO dispute panel had upheld an otherwise GATT-inconsistent measure on the basis of this exception.

Canada is currently appealing the panel decision in the Asbestos case.

Article XIII both excepts government procurement from the major GATS rules and mandates further negotiations to develop trade rules in this area. This exception pertains to purchasing of services for the direct use of government agencies. It would probably apply, for instance, to hospital dietary and laundry services procured on contract by a regional health authority. These services are excluded from the most favoured nation (MFN), national treatment and market access provisions of the GATS. Subsidies or grants to health services providers are not considered procurement and would not benefit from this exclusion.[5]

Most favoured nation (MFN) rule

The MFN rule (article II) applies to all services except those shielded by the narrow Article I:3 exclusion. This rule requires governments to "immediately and unconditionally" accord the best treatment given to *any* foreign service or service provider to *all* like foreign services and service providers.

MFN is a powerful provision that already applies to the Canadian health care sector. Once foreign provision of a given service is established through any of the four GATS modes of supply, a government measure cannot discriminate between foreign services or providers that are considered to be "like." For instance, a government cannot differentiate between the service provided by a foreign-owned private lab located in Toronto (mode 3) and a lab which provides a "like" diagnostic service remotely from Europe (mode 1).

The reach of this rule, and of the national treatment rule, has been extended by WTO dispute panel interpretations regarding how "likeness" is established and what constitutes discriminatory treatment. These are discussed below in relation to national treatment.

Although Canada, like other nations, has scheduled certain country-specific exceptions to the MFN rule, none of these relate to health services.[6] (All listed exceptions are subject to review; no new exceptions are permitted.)

Monopolies and state enterprises

The GATS rules regarding monopolies (Article VIII) appear, with the MFN rule in the section of the agreement titled "General Obligations and Disciplines." Article VIII.1, requires that all services provided by a monopoly provider comply with the MFN rule. As in Article II, this obligation applies generally, to unlisted as well as listed services.

Other features of Article VIII apply only to listed services. Article VIII.2 provides that "where a monopoly supplier competes, whether directly or through an affiliated company, in the supply of a service outside the scope of its monopoly rights and which is subject to that Member's specific commitments, the member shall ensure that such a supplier does not abuse its monopoly position to act in its territory in a manner inconsistent with such commitments."

Article VIII.4 concerns the possibility that a member country may grant monopoly rights to provide a service that is covered by its specific commitments. It requires the country to negotiate trade compensation with any other country whose commercial interests may be affected by the new monopoly rights, and if necessary to submit to arbitration.

Other general obligations

Article III, Transparency, requires member governments to make public any general measures relevant to the GATS rules. Governments are also required to respond promptly to all requests from another member government for specific information.

Article VI, Domestic Regulation, targets general, non-discriminatory regulation. All measures of general application affecting trade in services "must be administered in a reasonable, objective and impartial manner." Governments are also required to establish, where they do not already exist, administrative tribunals or procedures through which foreign service suppliers can appeal "administrative decisions affecting trade in services." Even more controversially, Article VI also requires that a broad range of measures, including technical standards and licensing requirements, "are not more burdensome than necessary to ensure the quality of the service."

This potentially formidable restriction on governments' regulatory ability already applies provisionally in sectors where governments have made specific commitments. Article VI.4 also commits member countries to negotiations to develop further restrictions on non-discriminatory domestic regulation –which would enormously increase the power of the WTO to interfere with non-discriminatory "behind-the-border" measures. According to the WTO Secretariat, new rules on domestic regulation are intended to apply to any service sector, not only those for which country-specific commitments have been made. These negotiations, are discussed further in section 3.2.2.

Market Access and National Treatment rules

Certain GATS rules, of which the most important are Article XVI, Market Access, and Article XVII, National Treatment, apply only to sectors in which countries have made specific commitments. (Canada's schedule of specific commitments is discussed below.)

Market access

Article XVI prohibits a wide range of "numerical restrictions" regulating access by scheduled services to a national or regional market. Prohibited restrictions include limits to the number of service suppliers, quotas limiting the total value of services provided, quotas limiting the number of people employed to provide a service, and restrictions on the type of legal entity permitted to provide a service – all of which are important measures for controlling costs and ensuring access to publicly funded health services. Limits on foreign ownership are also prohibited.

These are absolute prohibitions that apply whether or not such measures discriminate between domestic and foreign service providers. They could have significant implications for health insurance, a service which Canada has scheduled. They could impair the ability of Canadian governments to prevent escalating costs from undermining a major expansion of Medicare coverage (see section 4.1).

National treatment

Article XVII requires member governments to accord to foreign services and service providers treatment no less favourable than it accords to "like" domestic services and service providers.

As mentioned above, the reach of this rule, and of the MFN rule, has been extended by WTO dispute panel interpretations regarding how "likeness" is established and what constitutes discriminatory treatment.

The GATS is designed to prevent governments from distinguishing between services or service providers on the basis of how a service is provided. This principle of "modal neutrality" was given a very forceful interpretation in the Auto Pact case (in which a complaint against Canada was upheld). The WTO panel ruled that the mode of supply is irrelevant in determining "likeness" of a service or service provider. For the purpose of determining likeness, therefore, it is not relevant whether a hip operation, for instance, is provided in a for-profit clinic in Houston or in a public hospital in Edmonton. Or whether a cancer specialist diagnoses a brain tumor in a Canadian patient by viewing an MRI image remotely from her Philadelphia office, or in person at the Sudbury cancer clinic.

This strong interpretation of "modal neutrality" appears to be widely accepted and will be increasingly influential given the proliferation of telehealth applications. Two leading experts on the GATS and electronic commerce comment that, "electronic commerce is likely to be where disputes arise" regarding the issue of "likeness," which "has become one of the most contentious in the WTO for both goods and services." In their view the rules are unequivocal:

> Clearly a given electronic service should be treated the same whether it is delivered from home or abroad. But should a service that is delivered electronically from abroad be treated in the same manner as one that is delivered domestically

> *through nonelectronic means? The technologi-*
> *cal neutrality requirement would dictate that*
> *there is no reason for differential treatment.*[7]

The GATS national treatment rule is given added force because it incorporates a far-reaching view of what constitutes discriminatory treatment. Article XVII.3 specifies that a measure that treats foreign and domestic services identically may still be found to be discriminatory "if it modifies the conditions of competition in favour of services or services suppliers of the Member compared to like services or service suppliers of any other Member." In other words, it maintains that formally identical treatment can nevertheless result in *de facto* discrimination "if it modifies the conditions of competition" in favour of domestic services or service providers. In the EC Bananas case, the Appellate Body applied this interpretation to the MFN rule, further entrenching this tough standard of *de facto* discrimination.[8]

Given the diversity of national health systems, where health services are covered by the national treatment rule, there is enormous potential for Canadian measures to be found to effectively alter the conditions of competition in favour of domestic services or service providers. For example, an otherwise non-discriminatory requirement that providers of a particular health service be not-for-profit entities, or that restricts public funding to not-for profit providers, could be construed, in effect, to favour Canadian providers over U.S. providers, who are predominantly for-profit entities.

Classification and Coverage of Canadian Health Services

How services are classified is important to understanding the implications of the GATS because not all the services that make up Canada's health system are classified as health services within the classification system used in the GATS negotiations. Therefore some health services may already be covered by Canadian commitments which apply GATS disciplines in other service sectors.

"Health-related and social services" (Sector 8 of the WTO Sectoral Classification) includes the following components of our health system: hospital services, long-term care facilities, ambulance services, public health programs, (and possibly labs/diagnostic services, and health protection/monitoring and surveillance). These services are not included in Canada's schedule of specific commitments.

"Business services" (Sector 1) includes the sub-sector "Professional services" which include: physician services, dental services, and services of other health professionals, including mid-wives, nurses and physiotherapists, and paramedical personnel (which may include chiropractors, naturopaths, Aboriginal healers and other providers of complementary health services). These services provided by health professionals are also not included in Canada's schedule of specific commitments, although certain other professions are listed.

Services provided in private clinics may be classified in either of the two above categories. The distinguishing feature, according to the WTO Secretariat, is the presence of institutional nursing services.[9] If nurses are employed within the facility, it is considered to provide a hospital service, or other category under Sector 8 "health-related and social services." If not, it is considered a category of professional health service under Sector 1 "business services."

This distinction also applies to Home care, which involves the work of nurses, occupational therapists and other professionals in non-institutional settings. Therefore their services would in all likelihood be classified as a category of professional health services within the "business services" sector. The legal status of the service provider (e.g., not-for-profit vs private for-profit) is not a factor in determining the classification of the service.

Health insurance is categorized, together with life and accident insurance, as an "insurance and insurance related service" within Sector 7 "financial services." Canada has scheduled these services. As elsewhere, no distinction is made between public, not-for-profit and private, commercial providers of health insurance. The implications of Canada's commitments regarding health insurance are discussed in the next chapter.

The precise classification of other health services is difficult to determine. Health information may be classified under several possible categories of "business service" (e.g., "computer and related services," "research and development services," or "other business services"), some but not all of which Canada has scheduled. They could also be classified as one or other category of "telecommunication services" which Canada has scheduled. Health protection, surveillance and monitoring services could be a category of either "research and development services" or of "other human health services," neither of which Canada has scheduled.

Telehealth applications could be classified variously, depending on the particular service provided through this medium.

Table 5
Canada's Health System and the WTO Sectoral Classification List

Major Components of Canada's Health System	Corresponding WTO Sectoral Classification (* **bold text** indicates services classifications listed in Canada's current schedule of specific commitments, i.e. those subject, with some limitations, to the GATS market access and national treatment disciplines)		
	Sector 1 Business Services	Sector 8 Health Related and Social Services	Other Sectors
Health insurance			**"Life, accident and health insurance services" classified under the Financial Services sub-sector, "All insurance and insurance related services."** CPC 8121 (81291)
Hospital services	**"building cleaning services" CPC code 874**	Hospital services CPC 9311	
Physician Services	"Medical and dental services" classified under sub-sector for Professional Services CPC 93121 (generalists), 93122 (specialists)		
Services provided in private for-profit clinics	Likely classified as either "hospital service", if care involves institutional nursing, or as "medical and dental service" if no institutional nursing is present.		
Dental/optometry care	"Medical and dental services" are classified under Professional services sub-sector of Business Services. CPC 93123 No classification found for Optometry		
Pharmacists	Likely included in the classification for "Services provided by midwives, nurses, physiotherapists and para-medical personnel," under the Professional services sub-sector of Business services. CPC 93191		
Non-prescription drugs			Sales of non-prescription drugs are likely classified as "retailing services" under Sector 4 Distribution services. CPC 631+632, 6111+6113+6121

Services of other professionals (incl. mid-wives, psychologists, physiotherapists, chiropractors, private duty nurses)	"Services provided by midwives, nurses, physiotherapists and paramedical personnel" under the Professional Services sub-sector of Business Services. CPC 93191	
Alternative/Complementary health (incl. traditional Aboriginal healers, naturopaths, homeopaths, practitioners of oriental medicine)	Some may be classified as "Services provided by midwives, nurses, physiotherapists and paramedical personnel" under the Professional Services sub-sector of Business Services. CPC 93191	Other services may be classified as "retailing services" under Sector 4 Distribution services. CPC 631+632, 6111+6113+6121
Long-term care (residential)		"Residential health facilities services other than hospital services" under the "Other human health services" sub-sector of Health Related and Social Services. CPC 93193
Home care	"Services provided by midwives, nurses, physiotherapists and paramedical personnel" under the Professional Services sub-sector of Business Services. CPC 93191	
Ambulance services		"Ambulance services" under "Other human health services" sub-sector of Health Related and Social Services CPC 93192
Public health programs		"Other human health services not elsewhere classified" under the "Other human health services" sub-sector of Health Related and Social Services. CPC 93199

Table 5 continued			
Major Components of Canada's Health System	Sector 1 Business Services	Sector 8 Health Related and Social Services	Other Sectors
Laboratories/Diagnostic services		"Other human health services not elsewhere classified" (includes "morphological or chemical pathology, bacteriology, virology, immunology etc., and services n.e.c., such as blood collection services) under "Other human health services" sub-sector of Health Related and Social Services CPC 93199	
Health information services	Could be classified under any of the following Business Services: Computer and Related Services (including **"data processing" CPC 84300; or "data base services" CPC 844**); or Research and Development Services (including "natural sciences" CPC 851; **"social sciences and humanities" CPC 852**; and "interdisciplinary" CPC 853); or **Other Business Services (which includes "related scientific and technical services" CPC 8675)**		Could be classified in the **Communication Services** sector as **Telecommunication Services sector (which includes "on-line information and database retrieval" CPC 7523, and "on-line information and/or dataprocessing" CPC 843).**
Health protection: monitoring and surveillance	Could be classified as "natural sciences" (CPC 851) under Research and Development Services sub-sector of Business Services.	Could be classified as "other human health services not elsewhere classified" (includes "morphological or chemical pathology, bacteriology, virology, immunology etc., and services n.e.c., such as blood collection services) under the Other Human Health Services sub-sector of Health Related and Social Services CPC 93199	
Telehealth applications	Could be classified as any of the above, depending on particular service provided through this medium		

Sources: WTO Council for Trade in Services, *Health and Social Services; background note by the Secretariat*, 18 September 1998 (S/C/W/50); United Nations, *Provisional Central Product Classification* (ST/FSA/STAT/SER.M/77); Shaila Nijhowne (Statistics Canada) and David Usher (DFAIT), *Classification, the Measurement of Production and International Trade in Services, and GATS*, Paper presented to the Preparatory Conference, Services 2000: New Directions in Services Trade Liberalization, Washington D.C., June 1-2 1999; and GATS, Canada: *Schedule of Specific Commitments* (15 April 1994, and subsequent revisions in supplements 2(rev.1), 3 and 4) GATS/SC/16.

Health services for First Nations and Inuit could also be classified variously, depending on the particular service in question.

Table 5 summarizes the WTO sectoral classifications which correspond to the major components of Canada's health system. Health insurance is the only health service listed in Canada's current schedule of specific commitments. Depending on how health information services are classified, they may also already be covered by Canada's commitments for certain classifications in the "business services" and "communication services" sectors.

The table demonstrates, however, that Canada's health services are classified under numerous different sectors within GATS classification system. Therefore, within each of these sectors there is potential for extending GATS coverage to a component of our health system through increasing Canada's commitments, reducing limitations on those commitments, or redefining the scope of services covered by a given classification.

Canada has entered certain "horizontal" limitations (country-specific exemptions) which apply to its specific commitments in any service sector. One of these limitations concerns the cost of health services provided to foreign investors. Canada has limited their right to national treatment, effectively allowing Canadian governments to require foreign investors to pay more than Canadian residents for health services. Another more general limitation provides that services supplied or subsidized "within the public sector" may differentiate between Canadians and foreign investors, and cannot be considered an advantage or subsidy covered by national treatment.[10] The meaning of this limitation for health services is unclear. The most straightforward interpretation is that foreign service pro-

viders (or their employees) who are denied access to public services based on their residency or nationality cannot
argue that this violates the GATS national treatment obligation.[11]

Specific commitments of other countries

Canada's negotiating partners at the GATS have made more
extensive commitments in health services. Table 6 shows
the number of countries which have included selected
health services in their initial schedules of specific commitments.[12]

Many of the countries represented in the table below
are developing countries with little commercial interest in
gaining access to Canada's health market. However, as the
following table shows, Canada's major trading partners
have also made considerably more commitments than
Canada. The United States and Japan have scheduled hospital services. Mexico, the European Community, Mexico
and Australia have scheduled the services of health professions and other health services, including long term care,
in addition to health insurance and hospital services.

These countries have considerable commercial interest
in gaining access to international health services markets,

Table 6 Overview of Commitments for Selected Health Services		
Sector	Number of Member Countries which have made some commitments	Number of member countries which have made full commitments*
Medical and dental services	49	12
Midwives, nurses, etc	26	4
Hospital services	39	9
Other human health services	13	6
*Full commitments for both market access and national treatment, applied to modes 1,2 and 3 (cross-border, consumption abroad and commercial presence) with no limitations on coverage. Source: WTO Council for Trade in Services, *Health and Social Services: background note by the Secretariat*, 18 September 1998 (S/C/W/50), p.27.		

	Health Insurance	Professional Services		Health-related services	
		Medical and dental	Midwives, nurses, etc.	Hospital services	Other health services
Canada	X				
United States	X			X	
Mexico	X	X	X	X	X
EC*	X	X	X	X	X
Japan	X			X	
Australia	X	X	X	X	X

Table 7
Specific GATS Commitments for Health Services, Canada and Major Trading Partners

*European Community (12 member countries)
Source: WTO Council for Trade in Services, *Health and Social Services: background note by the Secretariat*, 18 September 1998 (S/C/W/50), pp.24-5.

and can be expected to use their negotiating leverage at the GATS to seek further commitments by Canada. While the federal government insists it will make no further commitments in this area,[13], this position is impaired by its aggressive pursuit of increased access to the health services markets of other countries.

GATS 2000 negotiations:
How might GATS coverage of health services be extended?

Article XIX.1 of the GATS commits member to enter into successive rounds of negotiations "with a view to achieving progressively higher levels of liberalization." The GATS 2000 negotiations, which were officially launched in February, 2000, are the first such round of negotiations.

Although member countries agreed to have their negotiating positions prepared by December 2000, Canadian officials have indicated that Canada's negotiators may only have an "initial mandate" ready by March 2001 and that developing a full negotiating position will be an "incremental process." Unlike European countries, the Government of Canada does not intend to publicly release its detailed negotiating position publicly or request-offer lists.[14]

The GATS 2000 negotiations are expected to intensify after a mid-term "stock taking" exercise in March 2001 that is expected to begin the crucial "market access" phase of negotiations.

In these negotiations, Canada, along with other members of the Quad group (the U.S., Japan and the European Community) is working to accelerate the pace for extending GATS coverage. To supplement the incremental "request-offer" negotiating process, negotiators are proposing various "horizontal approaches" which would bind member countries to extending GATS rules across service sectors or commit them to achieving a specified level of coverage.

These approaches are designed to box elected governments into providing more market access than they would otherwise be prepared to provide. They may equip negotiators to make commitments in politically sensitive areas such as health care without drawing the public and political attention that would be raised by explicitly listing them in Canada's schedule of specific commitments. Or they may remove the flexibility built into the request-offer approach, which requires each country to positively list the services to which national treatment and market access rules apply.

Implicit in the discussion of horizontal negotiating approaches is the understanding that the price of progress in the GATS 2000 negotiations will be concessions which WTO members are able to make only if their negotiators are insulated from domestic political pressures. At the conclusion of the GATS 2000 negotiations, then, Canadians may well be told that our only choice is between accepting or rejecting a single final package in which gains for unrelated Canadian exports are bundled together with rules imposing commercial principles on crucial health services.

The following sections briefly summarize the main areas of negotiation and discuss how they might extend GATS coverage of health services.

Expanding market access commitments

The core of the GATS 2000 negotiations will be efforts to increase GATS coverage by expanding countries' specific commitments. This can be achieved by increasing the number and extent of specific commitments in national schedules, removing limitations on market access and national treatment within already committed sectors, and binding more new and existing commitments to prevent governments from reversing them in the future.

Canadian negotiators can expect to be under considerable pressure from other delegations to make more commitments in health services. Compared to its major trading partners Canada has made few commitments in this area (see section 3.1.3). Yet Canada is aggressively pursuing increased access to health markets in other countries, and pushing all member countries to significantly increase GATS coverage overall.

Classification issues provide Canada's delegation with a means of reconciling these negotiating pressures with the federal government's official position that it will resist all demands to increase Canada's commitments in health services. Negotiators are addressing numerous difficulties with the GATS classification system and attempting to reach agreement on a standard approach to classifying services in schedules of country-specific commitments. In their work to resolve these classification issues, negotiators can maximize coverage of services in several ways. These include:

narrowing the description of excluded sectors; disaggregating services; and clustering services.

Narrowing the description of excluded sectors

GATS coverage can be expanded by reducing the scope of services classifications in which member governments have taken the fewest commitments, and expanding the scope of services classifications in which members have taken the greatest commitments.

As Table 5 shows, Canada's health services are classified under various GATS service sectors, including business services (sector 1) and financial services (sector 7) as well as health-related and social services (sector 8). In several cases, a health service could be assigned to two or more different GATS services categories. Negotiators may agree, for instance, that management of health information systems should be categorized under "computer and related services," a sub-sector of business services which Canada has scheduled, rather than under "health-related and social services" which are not scheduled.[15] The result would be to extend GATS coverage in an area of growing significance for health care without making any change to Canada's schedule of commitments.

Disaggregating services

Another way of increasing coverage is to separate out sub-categories of service sectors in which member countries have taken few commitments. This would allow negotiators to make commitments in certain sub-categories while still assuring the public that the larger sector is not covered.

Ambulance services, for instance, are currently classified under "other human health services," a sub-category of "health-related and social services" for which Canada has made no commitments. By separating out ambulance services, negotiators could agree to subject them to GATS rules without listing the more general categories of health services. Canadian officials have advocated use of a more detailed classification system that would facilitate such an approach.[16]

Clustering of services

Another proposed technique would bundle together the various services involved in a commercial activity in which GATS negotiators are seeking increased coverage. Any subsequent commitments would then apply to the entire cluster, even though the various services might be classified under different categories or sectors. This approach has been proposed by American companies to achieve greater market access for express delivery and energy services.

Clustering could also be applied to telehealth applications, an area of growing commercial interest and the focus of Canada's International Business Strategy for promoting exports of health services. Because telehealth applications cut across the full spectrum of health services, any market access commitments made in this area would affect governments' ability to regulate in a wide range of health services – from the direct provision of information to individuals, to consultations with specialists, homecare assessments and diagnostic lab services.

Domestic regulation

The commitment to negotiate new rules on domestic regulation in all service sectors is the GATS' boldest innovation to extend its reach behind national borders. If these negotiations fulfill the ambitious aims written into Article VI, the GATS rules on domestic regulation will be as interventionist (and in some respects more interventionist) as the highly controversial NAFTA investment rules.

The GATS defines the government measures that would be restricted by these rules in very general terms to include "qualification requirements and procedures, technical standards and licensing requirements." Health measures that would be covered by this wide definition range from qualifications required for accreditation and certification of health professionals, to licensing of hospitals, health clinics and other facilities, to performance standards and codes of ethics for health practitioners.[17]

It is important to highlight that these measures need not be discriminatory in order to be found in violation of the proposed rules on domestic regulation. In fact, the terms of Article VI are designed to provide foreign investors and service providers with an avenue for challenging government measures which are fully consistent with the stringent non-discrimination requirements of the MFN and national treatment rules. A regulatory measure that treats domestic and foreign services and service providers equally could nevertheless be overturned if a WTO dispute panel rules that it is "more burdensome than necessary to ensure the quality of the service." In this respect the proposed rules would be a more potent restriction than the abused NAFTA investment chapter, which requires complainants to demonstrate that a regulatory measure "is tantamount to expropriation" in order to prove a violation.[18]

Article VI.2 provides for a dispute settlement mechanism that could, like the NAFTA investment chapter, enable individual foreign investors or service providers to directly challenge a government measure (as opposed to being represented by its national government). Article VI.2 requires member governments to maintain domestic tribunals and procedures to review administrative decisions and, "where justified," to assess appropriate remedies. In Canada and other countries where administrative review and appeal procedures are commonplace, it is anticipated that these powers would be conferred on existing bodies. The decisions of these domestic tribunals, such as the quasi-judicial Canadian International Trade Tribunal, are legally binding. In this respect they could provide an equally attractive avenue for foreign investors and service providers to challenge non-discriminatory government regulatory measures.

The proposed procedure for assessing whether a measure is in violation of the domestic regulation rules is sharply tilted against any constraints on commercial activity. The "necessity test" borrowed from the GATT requires a government to show first that the measure is necessary in order to achieve a WTO-sanctioned legitimate objective, and second that no less commercially restrictive alternative measure was possible. In the GATT this test is applied to measures which have been found to be discriminatory and which a government is seeking to shield under the article XX general exceptions. As previously mentioned, the French ban on asbestos products is the only such measure that has been shielded on health grounds in over 50 years of GATT jurisprudence – and Canada is appealing the WTO panel decision in this case. The proposed GATS restrictions, which already apply provisionally in scheduled sectors, transform the stringent "necessity test" shield into a sword, that can be used to attack entirely non-discriminatory, public interest regulation.

Publicly, Canadian negotiators maintain that negotiations at the GATS Working Party on Domestic Regulations are focusing exclusively on the regulation of a few professional services (accountancy, legal services, engineering and architectural services). The terms of Article VI, however, contain a much broader agenda, one that is also confirmed in discussion documents prepared by the WTO Secretariat. Canadian officials have acknowledged, under questioning, that the Working Party is in fact operating on "two tracks,"[19] the first of which concerns regulation of selected professional services and the second of which concerns developing restrictions on domestic regulations that could be applied across all service sectors. This sweeping agenda is also confirmed in a WTO document titled "GATS Article VI.4: disciplines on domestic regulation applicable to all services." It explains that the major challenge for the Working Party is to transform the general principles of Article VI.4 into legally enforceable disciplines which can be interpreted by dispute settlement panels.[20]

The outcome of the negotiations on domestic regulation is not predetermined, and could fall short of the ambitions of the WTO Secretariat. Nevertheless, it is alarming that member countries have agreed to contemplate, and to apply provisionally, restrictions which would subject domestic regulations – which in the case of Canada's health system involve a complicated and delicate balancing of public policy objectives and commercial interests – to review by non-elected bodies on the basis of rules which so clearly favour commercial interests. It is doubly alarming that the Government of Canada continues to work towards developing these rules without publicly acknowledging their profound significance.

New obligations: subsidies and procurement

Other areas of potentially far-reaching significance for health care are negotiations mandated to develop new rules on subsidies and procurement.

Unlike the GATT and NAFTA non-discrimination rules, which specifically exclude subsidies, the GATS MFN and national treatment rules apply to subsidies. In addition to this coverage, the framework agreement commits member governments to negotiating further rules on subsidies. Article XV.1 states, "Members recognize that, in certain circumstances, subsidies may have distortive effects on trade in services. Members shall enter into negotiations with a view to developing the necessary multilateral disciplines to avoid such trade-distortive effects."

The negotiations on subsidies are at a very preliminary stage and there appears to be considerable confusion, even among member governments, about the extent of existing GATS coverage of subsidies. For instance, nothing in the framework agreement prevents a company, which is based in one country and provides a service remotely to users in another country, from claiming a national treatment right to a subsidy received by domestic providers of a like service in the second country. The WTO Secretariat has given conflicting advice about whether, in this situation, the national treatment rule would require the government to compensate the service provider located outside its territory.[21] Such an eventuality would obviously have enormous consequences for any health service supported by public financial contributions or price supports. While the subsidies negotiations could conceivably develop means of shielding such measures, it is alarming that negotiators are mandated to develop further subsidies rules without first clarifying the full implications of existing coverage of subsidies.

As previously mentioned, GATS article XIII exempts government procurement from key GATS provisions, but also mandates further negotiations. These negotiations would be aimed at preventing governments from favouring local or national suppliers, and from negotiating commitments from service providers to transfer technology, purchase local goods and services, or provide offsets designed to promote domestic economic development. Because other WTO bodies are already addressing government procurement issues more broadly, there is, as yet, little momentum behind the GATS discussions in this area.

GATS rules on government procurement are most obviously relevant to health services such as hospital dietary and laundry services which are commonly provided on contract by commercial companies. Of relevance to a wider range of health services is how procurement is demarcated from grants and subsidies. The NAFTA defines procurement narrowly to mean government purchases "for the direct benefit and use of government entities." A wider definition could encompass some financial arrangements which would otherwise be considered grants or subsidies. Where this line is drawn between procurement and grants is especially critical because the GATS, unlike most other major commercial free trade agreements, fully covers subsidies and grants.

Chapter 4
Causes for Concern:
Implications for Specific Health Services

The previous chapter provided an overview of GATS implications for health care, examining first how existing GATS rules apply to health services, then how coverage of GATS rules may be extended in the GATS 2000 negotiations. This chapter focuses more closely on key components of Canada's health care system, allowing a more detailed discussion of specific concerns about the impact of existing GATS rules, and the potential impact of extended GATS coverage, on health services.

The following sections examine GATS implications for three critical components of the Canadian health care system: public health insurance, hospital services, and home care. While this analysis is not comprehensive, it suggests the full range of impacts that must be considered. The future of health care in Canada rests importantly on decisions about how health insurance, hospital services and home care are to be financed and delivered. International trade rules that greatly restrict governments' abilities to adapt and modify these services to meet changing needs and circumstances will significantly erode Canadian Medicare and preclude future options for health care reform.

Tables 8, 9 and 10 provide a summary of the analysis discussed in the following sections.)

Health Insurance

Astonishingly, Canada covered health insurance in its schedule of specific commitments in the Financial Services

sector. Moreover, negotiators "bound" Canada's commitments in the insurance sector, meaning all future government measures affecting health insurance services must be
GATS-consistent. Nothing in Canada's schedule excludes
public health insurance plans from its commitments in this
sector. Public health insurance is included in the services
classification referenced in Canada's schedule. Likewise,
although it had the opportunity to do so, Canada placed
no limitations on the application of the GATS MFN, national treatment or market access rules to public health insurance plans.

It is difficult to fathom why Canadian negotiators would
fully cover health insurance under the GATS, putting one
of Canada's most cherished social programs at risk. It is
even more difficult to understand why, having foolishly
opted to risk covering health insurance, they did not lodge
country-specific exceptions and limitations that might have
explicitly sheltered Canadian public health insurance from
GATS challenge.

Perhaps the most plausible explanation for Canadian officials' failure to explicitly exempt health insurance in Canada's schedule of commitments is that the Government of
Canada believes provincial health insurance plans are *a
priori* excluded under GATS Article I.3.[1] In the event of a
GATS dispute, Canada would now have to demonstrate
that provincial health insurance plans meet the Article I.3
criteria for a "a service in the exercise of governmental authority," namely that they are "a service which is supplied
neither on a commercial basis nor in competition with one
or more service suppliers."

As discussed below, a WTO dispute panel may find some
basis to question this assertion in recent provincial government initiatives to redefine the scope of insured health serv-

Table 8

Causes for Concern: Health Insurance

Relevant GATS classifications and corresponding CPC codes	GATS coverage of health insurance	Implications and Concerns
"Life, accident and health insurance services" (Financial Services Sector) • CPC code 8121: "Life insurance and pension fund services"* "Non-life insurance services" Financial Services Sector) • CPC code 8129: "non-life insurance services", • includes code 81291: "accident and health insurance services" *Canada's schedule repeats a cross-referencing error in the GATS classification list. However, Canada's GATS schedule includes both the appropriate GATS title and the appropriate CPC code for health insurance. Neither classification excludes public health insurance.	Both "life, accident and health insurance services" and "non-life insurance services" are entered in Canada's specific commitments in financial services: • Bound commitment to National Treatment and Market Access rules • Rules apply to governmental measures affecting health insurance provided by commercial presence (mode 3) • No health-related limitations to Canada's commitments General rules, including MFN, apply to government measures affecting health insurance provided by all modes of supply. Some ways GATS coverage could be extended: • Additional modes of supply (cross-border) • Domestic regulations Probable* basis for Federal Government assertion that health insurance is safeguarded from all GATS rules: • exclusion for services "provided in the exercise of governmental authority" (Article 1.3) • governments and other public entities are excluded from the definition of a "financial service supplier" (Annex on Financial Services) *(*The Government of Canada has not publicly explained its views on this matter. Nor did the author receive a substantive response to direct inquiries he made to senior government officials responsible for this file.)*	Bound commitments: NT and market access rules apply to all future government measures affecting the listed health insurance services. No limitations: No explicit protection for government measures affecting health insurance services. Weaknesses in protection of Medicare: • No explicit exclusion or definition of public health insurance; • Article 1.3 exclusion undermined by existence of some competition with commercial health insurers: e.g. delisted services; managed care initiatives; direct purchase of insured services by Workers' Compensation Plans. Undefined scope of protection for Medicare: • Even if Medicare is excluded, the ambit of this protection is likely to be limited to health services exclusively covered by public health insurance in 1994 (when Canada scheduled health services); • Subsequent government measures affecting insurance for other health services, e.g. home care or pharmacare, are unlikely to be protected (because Canada's commitments are bound). Restricted options for health reform: • Possible monopoly rights (Article VIII) challenge to any expansion of Medicare coverage to include health services currently covered by Canada's commitments, e.g. home care, pharmacare. • The risk of high compensation costs could deter any such initiative. • These rules would compromise governments' ability to ensure quality and cost-effectiveness: e.g. they could not limit public funding to not-for-profit home care providers, nor place limits on the number of service providers eligible for public funding.

ices and in practices of provincial Workers' Compensation plans.

Another more direct threat arises even if existing provincial health insurance plans are in fact excluded by Article I.3. Because Canada's commitments in health insurance are bound, GATS rules apply to all future government measures affecting the health insurance services listed in the Canadian schedule. In the absence of any definition of public health insurance in Canada's schedule (or elsewhere in the GATS), a WTO dispute panel could reasonably be expected to look to the health services that were exclusively covered by provincial health insurance plans in 1994 (when health insurance services were first listed in Canada GATS schedule). Insurance for all other health services – i.e., those covered only or partially by commercial health insurance in 1994 – would be considered included in the listing for health insurance in Canada's schedule. All future government measures affecting privately insured health services – which would in all probability include insurance for homecare, pharmaceutical drugs and long-term care – would be fully subject to GATS rules, including the onerous monopolies, national treatment and market access obligations.

Canada's options for health care reform will be significantly restricted if the scope of Article I.3 protection for public health insurance is limited, as feared. As discussed further below, it is not difficult to imagine a scenario in which future public health insurance initiatives might face a GATS challenge: for example, if, as has been actively considered, Canadian governments extend Medicare coverage to currently uninsured services such as homecare and pharmacare. A public initiative of this kind would effectively reduce the market for commercial health insurers.

Another WTO member could charge that expanding Medicare coverage is an extension of the public health insurance monopoly to a service covered by Canada's specific commitments, and so requires Canada to negotiate compensation with other WTO members before it is implemented.[2]

How is health insurance covered by the GATS?

There is nothing in Canada's GATS schedule, nor in the associated services classification system, which excludes provincial health insurance plans from Canada's financial services commitments.

Canada has listed "life, accident and health insurance services" among the financial services subject to NT and market access rules (in addition to MFN which applies to all services). [3]

As with most other financial services, Canada's commitments in health insurance cover commercial presence (i.e., services provided by foreign investors established in Canada) but not cross-border trade or consumption abroad.[4] Canada's commitments in health insurance are bound in accordance with the GATS Understanding on Commitments in Financial Services. This means that Canada cannot introduce future health insurance measures which are inconsistent with its GATS obligations. [5] [6]

In entering its financial services commitments, Canada repeated a cross-referencing error contained in the GATS classification list. Under its entry for "life, accident and health insurance" Canada referenced a classification (subclass 8121 of the United Nations Provisional Central Product Classification) which in fact covers life insurance and pension fund services, but not health insurance. Health insurance is included under a different CPC classification, 81291 ("accident and health insurance services"). Canada has also entered this classification in its Financial Services schedule, under the title "non-life insurance services."

Despite the listing error, it is clear that public health insurance is included in the definition of health insurance services listed in the Canadian schedule. Canada's GATS schedule includes both the specific title and the specific CPC code for health insurance. The CPC provisional description of this classification makes no distinction between public and commercial health insurance services.[7] In the Auto Pact case, the WTO panel ruled that errors or omissions in scheduling were not reason to limit or alter Canada's commitments once a service has been positively listed.[8]

It is disturbing that Canada's negotiators made basic listing errors, which remain uncorrected, in an area as politically sensitive as health insurance. This sloppiness heightens concern about the impact of the existing GATS and reinforces the need for greater transparency and vigilance in monitoring the work of Canadian officials in the GATS 2000 negotiations.

Canada had an opportunity when it was drafting its schedule to enter limitations that would shield provincial health insurance plans from its GATS commitments. Once a service has been positively listed in a bound commitment – as was health insurance – all government measures are subject to Canada's GATS commitments unless they are protected by specific limitations entered in the schedule. Canada's schedule, however, includes no such limitations on the application of NT and market access rules to provincial health insurance plans.[9] Nor does it include any exceptions restricting the application of the MFN rule.[10]

In short, Canada took none of the opportunities available to it to qualify or restrict its GATS commitments for health insurance, which is clearly defined to include public health insurance.

Does Article I.3 exclude public health insurance from the GATS?

It would be far-fetched to believe that Canadian negotiators simply overlooked the implications of listing health insurance services for Canada's health care system. The most plausible explanation for the lack of limitations on Canada's commitments in health insurance services is that the Government of Canada believed provincial health insurance plans are excluded *a priori* by GATS article I.3.

Commercial health insurers are prohibited from insuring hospital and medical expenses covered by public health insurance. This appears to satisfy the Article I.3(c) criteria for excluding existing provincial health insurance plans from the GATS, namely that they are "supplied neither on a commercial basis nor in competition with one or more service suppliers."[11]

The Government may also have believed that public health insurance was exempted by the Financial Services annex's definitions of "financial services" and "financial service providers" which explicitly exclude services provided by governments and other public entities "principally engaged in carrying out governmental functions or activities for governmental purposes."[12] This interpretation, if valid, would doubly shield *existing* public health insurance under Article I:3.

It is far from clear, however, that this protection extends to government initiatives to expand provincial health insurance coverage to a health service – such as home care or pharmaceuticals – which is now purchased privately, or by a combination of private and public funding. Private health insurance for home care and other health services outside Medicare fell within the scope of "financial services" at the time Canada entered its bound commitments covering health insurance services in 1994. Therefore, any subsequent government measures affecting these services are subject to GATS obligations. A GATS complainant might, as discussed below, successfully argue that public insurance of these services does not meet the criteria of Article 1.3 and is therefore fully subject to the GATS.

Possible GATS challenge

Numerous proposals for health care reform involve some expansion of the coverage of public health insurance. Expanded coverage of services such as home care, prescription drugs and long-term care could both address growing health needs which are unmet by the current hospital-based Medicare model and enable a more efficient use of resources by removing disincentives to use appropriate and more cost-effective health services.

Any such expansion of Medicare would effectively reduce the market for commercial health insurance plans which currently cover home care services, prescription drugs, and long-term care. Another WTO member could charge that this constitutes an extension of the public health insurance monopoly to a service which was part of the commercial health insurance market covered by Canada's specific GATS commitments. If such a challenge were successful, Canada would be required to negotiate compensation with other WTO members, or agree to an arbitration process, before extending Medicare coverage.[13]

The decisive issue for a WTO panel would likely be whether or not an extension of Medicare to previously uninsured health services meets the Article 1.3 criterion for "a service in the exercise of governmental authority." A complainant could argue that there is in fact a degree of competition between public and commercial health insurance providers, which weakens the Government of Canada's position that provincial health insurance plans are excluded under article 1.3. They could point to various initiatives to redefine the range of health services covered by provincial insurance plans. Since the early 1990s, provincial governments have removed certain services from provincial health plans, thereby incrementally expanding the market for commercial health insurers.

Moreover, several provinces have also experimented with "managed care" models in which physicians and health facilities are reimbursed by provincial health plans on a capitation basis rather than fee-for-service. The services supported by these payments are not restricted by the definition of insured health services, and in practice often include services such as physiotherapy, chiropractic and podiatry, which are normally purchased either by out-of-pocket payments or by private insurance plans. In practice, therefore, there is some intermingling in the coverage of commercial and public health insurance. A commercial health insurer, backed by a WTO member country, could maintain that this constitutes a degree of competition which disqualifies a provincial health insurance plan from protection under Article I.3.

To further support this line of argument, a GATS challenger could point to the practices of Workers' Compensation plans, which operate outside the Canada Health Act. In order to secure faster treatment for injured workers and speed their return to work, some provincial Workers' Compensation plans have directly purchased insured health services at publicly funded, not-for-profit hospitals.[14] In these circumstances, federal and provincial governments have in effect permitted Workers Compensation plans (which are attempting to reduce their wage replacement costs by seeking speedier medical treatment) to operate as parallel health insurance plans. This discrepancy in Medicare could be shown as further evidence that there is in fact a degree of competition between public and commercial health insurance providers, which weakens the claim that provincial health insurance plans are a "service in the exercise of governmental authority."

Even if Canada is able to demonstrate that provincial health insurance plans are not in competition with commercial health insurance, it would face a different and probably more difficult hurdle in invoking Article I.3 protection for new Canadian government initiatives to expand public health insurance. Because Canada's GATS commitments covering health insurance are bound, GATS rules apply to all future government measures affecting the health insurance services listed in the Canadian schedule.

In the absence of any definition of public health insurance in Canada's schedule (or elsewhere in the GATS), a WTO dispute panel could reasonably be expected to look to the health services that were exclusively covered by provincial health insurance plans in 1994 (when health insurance services were first listed in Canada GATS schedule). Insurance for all other health services – i.e., those covered only or partially by commercial health insurance – would be considered included in the listing for health insurance in Canada's schedule. All future government measures affecting this latter group – which would in all probability include insurance coverage for homecare, pharmaceutical drugs and long-term care – would be subject to the GATS national treatment and market access rules.

In the event of a GATS challenge to extending Medicare, a WTO dispute panel would be required to rule on the precise extent of Article I.3 protection for public health insurance, which is left undefined in Canada's schedule. Even if it excludes public health insurance from Canada's GATS commitments, a panel would have strong grounds for ruling that Canadian government measures affecting insurance for health services which were not covered by Medicare in 1994 – such as home care and prescription drugs – are fully subject to the GATS.

Canada's options for health care reform will be significantly restricted if the scope of Article I.3 protection for public health insurance is as limited as it appears to be. Another WTO member could charge that an expansion of Medicare coverage constitutes an extension of the public health insurance monopoly to a service covered by Canada's specific commitments, and so requires Canada to negotiate compensation with other WTO members before it is implemented. A successful GATS challenge would significantly increase the costs of expanding public health insurance. And even the risk of such a challenge could tilt the domestic policy debate against expanding Medicare to cover home care, prescription drugs, dental care, or other currently uninsured health services.

Another kind of GATS challenge could concern the data management and information processing which is central to health insurance services. Canada's GATS commitments in these areas could allow American health insurers to process claims and records remotely from their U.S. bases.

As discussed in chapter 3, health information services comprise a variety of different categories of services, several of which have been included in Canada's schedule of specific GATS commitments. These include business services such as "data processing" and "data base services" and communications services such as "on-line information and database retrieval" and "on-line information and/or dataprocessing" (see Table 5). Unlike health insurance, in which Canada's commitments apply only to commercial presence, Canada's commitments for these services apply to all modes of supply, with no limitations (other than those limiting the right of entry to Canada to managers and certain specialist occupations).

Based on these commitments, American health corporations present in the Canadian market could assert a GATS right to process Canadian health insurance claims and records remotely from their U.S. bases.[15] This would reduce the cost to U.S. health insurers of expanding their operations in Canada. By removing claims processing from Canadian jurisdiction, it would also create numerous regulatory and privacy concerns for provincial health ministries.

Potential for extended GATS coverage of health insurance

The risk of a GATS challenge would be even greater if the national treatment and market access rules were applied to foreign-based health insurance provided to Canadians by telephone, internet or other forms of cross-border supply (mode 1). As noted previously, limitations in Canada's schedule require foreign service providers to have a commercial presence within Canada in order to provide insurance services.

Ironically, a Government of Canada discussion paper proposes that one of Canada's objectives at the GATS 2000 negotiations be to extend member countries' commitments to different modes of supply. In a section on e-commerce, the same discussion paper notes:

> *Previous rounds of WTO negotiations on financial services have tended to focus on issues relating to establishment and commercial presence in financial markets. Increasingly, however, financial institutions will be able to service foreign markets from abroad, without having to establish a permanent commercial presence in the market.*[16]

If GATS coverage of insurance services were extended in this manner, it would vastly increase the number of commercial insurers with GATS-enforceable national treatment and market access rights to supply the Canadian market. As the fate of the Clinton health care reforms attest, increased rights for American for-profit health corporations would certainly influence Canadian health policy debates for the worse. The debate about how best to control Medicare costs could be tilted in favour of U.S.-style managed care. [17] The risk of being forced to compensate U.S.-based health insurers would discourage consideration of other policy options for containing costs within a single payer public insurance model — such as primary care reform and expanded coverage of preventive and community-based services.

The same Canadian discussion paper notes that financial services could be further liberalized by developments in the GATS 2000 negotiations on domestic regulations. Noting that financial services are highly regulated, it suggests Canada may seek rules restricting non-discriminatory regulations which hinder the provision of financial services by commercial presence or by cross-border supply.[18] As previously noted, the Canadian International Business Strategy for health services has identified a number of regulatory measures as "barriers to market access" for Canadian telehealth exports. These include licensure requirements (requiring a physician to be licensed in the jurisdiction in which the service is provided) and regulations preventing physicians from being compensated for services provided remotely from another jurisdiction.

A change to these regulations in Canada would require new approaches to limiting public health insurance costs. It is alarming that the Government of Canada is poised to target these regulations in other countries without acknowledging that it would be under strong pressure to agree to similar restrictions to Canadian health regulations, and without considering the implications for public health insurance at home or abroad.

Hospital Services

Because hospital services are not entered in Canada's schedule of specific commitments, they are not subject to the GATS national treatment and market access rules. To the extent that hospital services meet the Article I.3 criteria for "a service supplied in the exercise of governmental authority," they are also not covered by any other GATS rules, including MFN.

Table 9
Causes for Concern: Hospital Services

Relevant GATS classifications and corresponding CPC codes	GATS coverage of hospital services	Implications and Concerns
"Hospital Services" (Health Related and Social Services Sector) • CPC code 9311: "Hospital Services" • Services delivered under the direction of a medical doctor • No reference to food, laundry and custodial services provided in hospitals.	National Treatment and Market Access rules: • Medical services included in the definition of Hospital Services are not covered. • Hospital food services are covered if included in the "Hotels and Restaurants (including catering) classification. • Janitorial services are covered if included in the "Building cleaning services" classification.	National treatment rule restricts ability of hospitals (or regional health authorities) to "contract in" food, laundry or janitorial services: • Vulnerable to a GATS challenge, charging it modified the conditions of competition against foreign-owned service providers. • Canada would be required to ensure regional health authority reversed its decision, or provide compensation.
"Hotels and Restaurants (including catering)" (Tourism and Travel related services sector) • CPC code 64220: cafeteria services • CPC code 64230: catering services	MFN and other general rules: • Medical services in hospitals are protected as long as they are provided on a non-commercial basis and not in competition with private health facilities (Article I.3) • This protection is undermined by Alberta's legislation to permit public funding of private for-profit hospitals, and by more limited revenue-generating activities in other provinces.	MFN coverage of core hospital services would amplify the NAFTA implications of Alberta's legislation: • If the federal government does not act against Alberta, NAFTA national treatment rule could require it to permit any other province to fund insured surgical services provided by U.S.-based for-profit health corporations. • The GATS MFN obligation could extend the reach of the NAFTA national treatment rules by requiring Canadian governments to provide equally favourable treatment to all foreign based health corporations, including in regard to the provision of subsidies.
"Building clearning services" (Business Services sector) • CPC code 874: "building cleaning services" • Includes code 87403, "janitorial services" (No reference to laundry services found in GATS classification list or in CPC)	Some ways GATS coverage could be extended: • Domestic regulations • Government procurement • Subsidies	

However, certain activities within hospitals – including laundry, food and custodial services — are likely to be considered hotel and business services, which are covered by Canada's specific GATS commitments.

In addition, Alberta's legislation to allow commercial hospital care undermines the basis for an Article I.3 exclusion and is likely to expose Canadian hospital services to the general GATS rules including MFN. Certain revenue-generating activities of hospitals in other provinces may also already be subject to the GATS horizontal rules, including MFN.

How are hospital services covered by the GATS?

In order to determine which hospital activities are shielded from the national treatment and market access rules, a WTO dispute panel would consider which activities are classified as hospital services and which may be classified in other sectors in which Canada has made specific commitments.

A defining characteristic of "hospital services" in the UN Provisional Central Product Classification (on which the GATS Services Sectoral Classification List is based) is that they are provided under medical supervision:

> *Services delivered under the direction of medical doctors chiefly to in-patients, aimed at curing, reactivating and/or maintaining the health status of a patient. Hospital services comprise medical and paramedical services, nursing services, laboratory and technical services including radiological and anaesthesiological services, etc.*[19]

Therefore, Canadians can be confident that the GATS national treatment and market access rules do not apply to this broad range of medical services provided in hospitals.

The GATS and CPC classifications make no reference, however, to the food, laundry and custodial services provided within hospitals. In Canadian hospitals, these services are commonly provided by workers employed by a commercial contractor. There is a strong possibility a WTO dispute panel would consider these activities to be business and hotel services, which are subject to the national treatment and market access rules.

In its specific commitments covering "business services," Canada has entered "building cleaning services" and referenced CPC classification 874, which includes janitorial services:

> *Services consisting in cleaning and maintaining dwellings and other buildings. Included here are floor cleaning and waxing, interior wall cleaning, furniture polishing and other janitorial and maintenance services.*[20]

In its schedule under "tourism and travel related services," Canada has entered "hotels and restaurants (including catering)." The definitions of the associated CPC classifications could reasonably be interpreted to include both hospital catering services and cafeterias[21]:

> *CPC prov code 64220 – Meal serving services in self-service facilities:*

> *Food preparation and serving services and related beverage serving services furnished by eating facilities that provide a range of pre-cooked foods from which the customer makes individual selections and is billed accordingly. These facilities provide seating but not individual waiter service; they are often known as cafeterias.*

> *CPC prov code 64230 – Caterer services, providing meals to outside:*

> *Food preparation and serving services provided by caterers to groups, on the premises or elsewhere. Included are beverage related services.*

No CPC classification for laundry services could be found.

Does Article I.3 exclude Canadian hospital services from the GATS?

Hospital services are not subject to the GATS' horizontal rules if they can be shown to meet the Article I.3 criteria that they "are a service which is supplied neither on a commercial basis nor in competition with one or more service suppliers." Because these criteria are contextual and there is great variation in how national health systems are funded and delivered, the scope of this exclusion may well differ from country to country, and even from province to province.

As long as the Canada Health Act is enforced, the insured health services provided within hospitals are shielded by Article I.3. The Act requires that provincial health insurance plans be publicly administered, on a non-profit basis, and that they provide universal access to all medically necessary services provided within hospitals. Virtually all hospitals are not-for-profit entities governed by a community-based board of directors and accountable to a public authority.[22] The vast majority of hospital services, therefore, are provided on a non-commercial basis and not in competition with other providers.

This protection from the GATS is undermined, however, by such reforms as Alberta's legislation to allow commercial hospitals to provide insured health services. The legislation allows commercial, for-profit hospitals to receive provincial health insurance fees for certain surgical services for which patients are charged an additional amount, paid either out-of-pocket or through private insurance.[23] Since part of the Alberta government's rationale for the legislation is to introduce private competition into the health system, these would in all likelihood enter into competition with each other and with not-for-profit hospitals. Therefore, these hospital services may no longer meet the Article I.3 criterion for "a service supplied in the exercise of governmental authority," and could be subject to the general GATS rules, including MFN.

Hospitals throughout Canada are increasingly providing certain revenue-generating activities which may be considered to be commercial activities in competition with other health providers. These include rehabilitative services paid by Workers Compensation plans and by private insurers. These hospital services could also be subject to MFN and other general GATS rules.

Possible GATS challenges

Food and other support services provided within hospitals are currently vulnerable to a GATS challenge. In addition, the Alberta private hospital legislation paves the way for a GATS challenge involving a wider range of hospital services.

Food, laundry and custodial services require a substantial on-site presence which limits opportunities for supplying these services through international trade. In practical terms, "trade" in laundry and custodial services is in most cases limited to "commercial presence" (i.e., provision by a foreign investor established in Canada). Meals, on the other hand, can be prepared off-site and can conceivably be transported across borders. Food services are the area of greatest commercial interest and are most likely to be the subject of a GATS challenge. A number of large Canadian- and foreign-owned companies – including Baxter, Bitove, Sodexho, Versa — compete to provide food services in Canadian hospitals.

A regional health authority which decided to revert to in-house provision of food services could be exposed to a GATS challenge. Such a situation could arise in regions where the privatization of hospital food services has been accompanied by increased mechanization and consolidation of food preparation in large central plants which provide ready-prepared meals to individual hospitals. The dietary quality and cost-effectiveness of these food operations have been widely questioned. (In one infamous case, a caterer transported bread that had been cooked in a Toronto plant to New Brunswick hospitals.)[24]

The complainant could charge that a decision to provide hospital food services in-house violates the GATS national treatment rule by modifying the conditions of competition against foreign-owned caterers.[25] If direct and contract provision of food services are considered to be "like" services, a WTO dispute panel could rule that a decision to bring food services in-house unfairly favours Canadian service providers. Canada would then be required to either reverse the decision of the regional health authority (which is outside federal government jurisdiction) or to provide compensation.

Commercial health corporations seeking to take advantage of Alberta's private hospital legislation could use the GATS in tandem with NAFTA to gain greater access to potentially lucrative sources of public spending throughout Canada. If the federal government permits domestically owned commercial hospitals to operate under the Alberta legislation, Canada's NAFTA reservation for health and social services could be undermined and a NAFTA national treatment right triggered. One jurist has argued that this would enable American-based commercial health corporations to claim a right throughout Canada to the same treatment as domestic commercial hospitals receive in Alberta, i.e., the right to bill provincial health insurance plans for insured surgical services.[26] In effect, by not intervening in the Alberta case, the federal government forfeits its right to intervene to prevent similar practices in other provinces.

If NAFTA provides commercial health care providers with a foot in the door of the Canadian health care system (the right to establish), the GATS may amplify *all* their rights once *any* are established. As noted above, the Alberta legislation weakens Canada's position that hospital services are excluded from the GATS under Article I.3. General GATS rules which could apply to hospital services include the powerful MFN provision.

Unlike NAFTA, the GATS applies to subsidies and grants. To the extent that MFN applies to hospital services, Canadian governments are required to provide equally favourable treatment to all foreign-based companies providing these services to the Canadian market. Foreign health corporations located outside Canada — for example, in Europe or in other WTO member countries — are entitled to the same treatment as foreign-based health corporations established within Canada. Similarly, U.S.-based corporations which gain access to the Canadian market through the NAFTA national treatment obligation could, once established, use the WTO MFN obligation to claim a right to receive the same level of subsidy or other advantages provided to any other foreign-based health corporation.

This interaction of NAFTA and GATS obligations could open the door to a potentially ruinous trade challenge. The modal neutrality principle stipulates that GATS rules apply to all "like" services and service providers, without regard to the mode of supply of the service. Commercial hospitals which treat Canadians in facilities located in the U.S. (or Mexico) – i.e., supply their services through "consumption abroad" — could conceivably challenge any Canadian government measure that restricts public funding or other advantages for insured services to commercial facilities located in Canada (i.e., those which supply their services through the commercial presence mode). A successful challenge could give a virtually unlimited number of commercial hospitals beyond Canada's borders a claim on Canada's public funding for health care, exposing Canada to trade retaliation and potentially overwhelming the capacity of provincial and federal governments to contain costs and regulate the quality of care.

This result would obviously be ruinous for the public interest. It may seem far-fetched and unlikely, but the logic of Canada's GATS and NAFTA obligations makes such a trade challenge possible. And, as recent events have shown, rulings of WTO trade tribunals have often exceeded even our worst fears.

Potential for extended GATS coverage of hospital services

Domestic political concerns will likely lead the Government of Canada to resist any pressure to list hospital services in its schedule of specific commitments. Nevertheless, the GATS 2000 negotiations provide a number of other indirect means of extending GATS coverage in this area.

The sweeping mandate of the negotiations on domestic regulation could include a review of the requirements and procedures for granting hospital charters and for recognizing professional qualifications required to practice in a hospital.[27] Other regulations which could be exposed to challenge as "more burdensome than necessary," include conditions limiting provincial funding to not-for-profit hospitals.

As contracted hospital services account for a large share of provincial and local government procurement, they would be of considerable interest in negotiations on government procurement, which are mandated by Article XIII and are expected to proceed either within the GATS or another WTO body.

The GATS also mandates further negotiations on subsidies (Article XV). These negotiations are complicated by the confusion surrounding existing GATS coverage of subsidies. Unlike NAFTA, the GATS rules already apply to subsidies. Without any definition of how national treatment and market access rules apply to subsidies, the GATS framework agreement could be interpreted very expansively.[28] Any efforts to limit the application of GATS rules to subsidies will be counterbalanced in the negotiations by commercial and national interests in using the GATS to gain access to potentially lucrative sources of public revenue.

Home Care

Home care services involve the work of professionals – including nurses, occupational therapists, and physiotherapists – and other workers, including homemakers, housekeepers, personal attendants and drivers.[29] Outside Manitoba, where home care is provided by provincial government employees, most home care workers are employed by private agencies. While these agencies have traditionally been not-for-profit, commercial provision of homecare has expanded following legislation in Ontario to permit public funding of for-profit agencies.

Total spending on home care in Canada has been estimated at $3.4 billion, of which 79% is from public sources.[30] As previously noted, there is strong commercial interest in home care services due to projections of high growth in spending in this area.

Home care services are not listed in Canada's schedule and therefore are not subject to the GATS national treatment and market access rules. They are, however, likely covered by the GATS general obligations, including MFN.

Given the strong commercial interest in home care, there may be pressure to extend GATS coverage of Canadian homecare services in the GATS 2000 negotiations. This could be accomplished by direct listing, reclassification or other means. Canadians should be wary of any such initia-

Table 10
Causes for Concern: Home Care

Relevant GATS classifications and corresponding CPC codes	GATS coverage of home care	Implications and Concerns
"Services provided by midwives, nurses, physiotherapists, and para-medical personnel" (Professional Services grouping within Business Services sector) <ul><li>CPC code 93191, "Deliveries and related services, nursing services, physiotherapeutic and para-medical services"</li></ul> "Other services not included elsewhere" <ul><li>Includes CPC code 98, "Private households with employed persons"</li><li>May apply to non-professional home care services, e.g. housekeeping</li></ul>	National treatment and market access rules do not apply to professional home care services. But MFN and other general GATS rules most likely do apply: <ul><li>Publicly funded home care unlikely to be excluded under Article 1.3</li><li>Scope of exception for government procurement is unclear, but NAFTA approach would not shield government contracts to agencies providing home care to the public.</li></ul> Some ways GATS coverage could be extended: <ul><li>Added to Canada's specific commitments</li><li>Reclassification of home care services</li><li>New classification for telehealth services</li></ul>	The MFN provision equips foreign-owned providers to accelerate the commercialization of home care in Canada. MFN requires that the most favourable treatment given to any foreign service or service provider be given "immediately and unconditionally" to *any and all* foreign services or service providers. This allows all home care providers to claim a right to the most advantageous deal given to any single foreign-based providers. MFN rule and modal neutrality principle could restrict governments' ability to regulate telehealth applications in home care: <ul><li>Conditions for public funding of telehealth applications -- e.g. video assessment and monitoring of home care patients -- could have a differential impact on commercial providers from different WTO member countries.</li><li>A successful MFN challenge would give foreign-owned companies providing remote telehealth services form outside Canada (cross-border supply) same access to public contracts as foreign-owned companies based in Canada (commercial presence).</li></ul> Extension of market access and monopolies rules to home care would restrict options for health reform: <ul><li>The market access rules (article XVI.2(e)) could prevent governments from providing public funding only to not-for-profit home care providers.</li><li>The monopolies rules (article VIII) could deter governments from directly providing home care services that were previously contracted to commercial providers.</li><li>These restrictions would limit the ability of governments to provide publicly funded home care services in the most cost-effective manner.</li></ul>

GATS Classifications: WTO, *Services Sectoral Classification List* (MTN.GNS/W/120, 10 July 1991).
CPC codes: United Nations, *Provisional Central Product Classification 1991* (ST/ESA/STAT/SER.M/77)
Legend: MFN – most-favoured-nation treatment; NT – National Treatment

tives, which would expose public policy on home care to potential GATS challenges.

How is home care covered by the GATS?

In the GATS classification system, home care services are a component of professional services within the business services sector. Thus, although Canada has not listed home care services in its specific commitments, they are grouped separately from hospitals, community clinics and other health services to which they may be administratively and financially linked. This separation increases the potential for extending GATS coverage of home care services independently of other health care services.

Home care services fall within the GATS classification for "services provided by midwives, nurses, physiotherapists and para-medical personnel." This category is distinguished from professional medical and dental services, which are also classified as professional services within the business services sector.[31]

As the description of the corresponding CPC classification shows, this grouping includes a diverse range of health occupations:

> Services such as the supervision during pregnancy and childbirth and the supervison of the mother after birth. Services in the field of nursing (without admission) care, advice and prevention for patients at home, provision of maternity care, children's hygienics, etc. Physiotherapy and para-medical services are services in the field of physiotherapy, ergotherapy, occupational

therapy, homeopathy, accupuncture, nutrition instruction, etc.[32]

The conditions of employment of home care providers are very different from those of other providers included in the same grouping. For instance, most practitioners of complementary medicine, such as homeopathy and accupuncture, are self-employed and are paid directly by individual patients.

The services of non-professional home care providers such as housekeepers and drivers may be classified in a residual category, "other services not included elsewhere." This GATS classification includes services in "private households with employed persons" (CPC code 98).

Does Article I.3 exclude home care services from the GATS?

Home care, as it is currently provided in Canada, would be unlikely to be considered "a service provided in the exercise of governmental authority." Although most home care services are funded publicly, they are provided by private agencies, including for-profit companies. These agencies typically compete with each other in the contracting process for publicly funded home care, and for privately paid services.

The classification of home care as a business service, not a health service, would also be considered if a WTO panel were required to rule on this issue.

Government procurement

It is not clear whether government contracting of home care services would be considered to be government procure-

ment, which is shielded from the GATS MFN, national treatment and market access rules.[33] The GATS does not define
procurement. And there are different approaches among
WTO members to defining the scope of government procurement. NAFTA countries, including Canada, have employed a narrow definition which generally includes only
government purchases of goods and services "for the direct benefit and use of government entities."[34] NAFTA's
procurement chapter specifies that "procurement does not
include "non-contractual agreements or any form of government assistance, including cooperative agreements,
grants, loans, equity infusions, guarantees, fiscal incentives,
and *government provisions of goods and services to persons or
state, provincial and regional governments (emphasis added)*."[35]
Such a definition may include home care services purchased
for convalescing government employees, but would probably exclude contracts to agencies for the provision of home
care to the general public.

Defining government procurement will be one of the
central issues in the negotiations mandated by GATS Article XIII. As Sinclair notes, "the more narrowly procurement
of services is defined in the GATS context, the narrower is
the scope of the existing Article XIII exemption. Where the
line is drawn between procurement and grants, for example, is especially critical in the GATS context because the
GATS, unlike most other major commercial free trade agreements, fully covers subsidies and grants."[36] The negotiations are also intended to lead to agreement on GATS rules
applying to government procurement.

Pending the outcome of these negotiations, it is unclear
whether or not contracts for publicly funded home care
would be shielded by the GATS exception for government
procurement.

Potential for extended GATS coverage of home care

Strong commercial interest in home care could lead to pressure in the GATS 2000 negotiations to further extend GATS coverage of home care.

This could be accomplished by securing specific commitments from additional countries. Twenty-six WTO members, including the European Union and Mexico, have listed home care services in their schedules of specific commitments (see tables 6 and 7). Canada can be expected to face pressure to also make commitments in this area.

Coverage could also be extended by altering the GATS classification of home care services. Services specific to home care could be separated from other services of less commercial interest. As noted above, the relevant GATS classification includes a disparate group of services. Disaggregating this grouping might add clarity to the GATS classification system. It could also facilitate scheduling of home care by additional WTO members.

Home care could also be affected if a GATS classification is created for telehealth services. As previously discussed, this "clustering" approach has been proposed for other services (see section 3.2.1). A classification which grouped all telehealth services would include remote monitoring and assessments of home care patients. As previously noted, industry sources predict strong growth for these and other telehealth applications in home care (see section 2.3).

Possible GATS challenges

If home care is not shielded by either Article I.3 or XIII, it is subject to the GATS general rules, including the obligation to provide most-favoured-nation treatment to all WTO members.

There are numerous commercial home care providers active in Canada, including a number of large corporations such as ParaMed, Bayshore Health Group and We Care. The vast majority of these companies' revenue comes from public health care budgets. For instance, ParaMed's operations are 90% funded by government, according to the president of is parent company.[37] Another WTO member country could initiate a GATS challenge on behalf of international investors with holdings in any of these corporations.

It is unlikely that a Canadian government would discriminate between foreign commercial home care providers on the basis of the nationality of their majority owners. However, in the give and take of government contracting and especially in the various privatization initiatives underway in certain Canadian provinces, foreign service providers will sometimes strike a deal on terms favourable to them. The GATS MFN provision requires that the most favourable treatment given to any foreign service or service provider be given "immediately and unconditionally" to *any and all* foreign services of service providers. As such, it is a powerful instrument for generalizing and consolidating these privatization and commercialization initiatives.

The possibility of an MFN challenge also arises with the adoption of telehealth applications in home care. The GATS doctrine of "modal neutrality" requires that a government not differentiate between services and service suppliers on the basis the mode of provision of the service. In principle, therefore a Canadian government is required to give the same level of treatment to a foreign-based firm providing aspects of home care service remotely (cross-border supply) as it provides to a foreign firm established in Canada (commercial presence).

An MFN case could arise if a Canadian government sets conditions for home care services provided remotely – the assessment and monitoring of patients, for instance – which are different from the requirements for the same home care services provided locally. A complainant could charge that these conditions have a differential impact on WTO member countries if, for instance, American-owned home care firms are established in Canada but European-owned firms are not. This differential treatment, a complaint would argue, is inconsistent with Canada's obligation to extend most-favoured-nation treatment to the services and service providers of all WTO members.

Canadian government policies regarding the delivery of home care services, as well as their financing, would be further restricted if GATS coverage is extended in the GATS 2000 negotiations. The discussion of health insurance (section 4.1) considered the basis for a possible GATS challenge to extending Medicare coverage to include home care. Conditions on how publicly funded home care services are provided could also be open to challenge from commercial home care companies.

Permitting commercial companies to provide home care services is a recent and controversial experiment in Canada. In Ontario the privatization of home care services has been accompanied by escalating costs, reduced financial accountability, and concerns about the availability and quality of the services provided.[38] In light of this experience, a future provincial government may very plausibly wish to return to the previous policy of funding only not-for-profit home care providers.

The GATS market access rules would obstruct such a change in policy. A foreign-owned company could challenge it on the basis that a restriction of publicly funded home care to not-for-profit agencies violates Article XVI.2(e) which prohibits measures "which restrict or require specific types of legal entity or joint venture through which a service supplier may supply a service." As this is an absolute prohibition on such measures, it would not be necessary for a complainant to show that this condition is discriminatory to foreign-owned firms. A WTO panel could require Canada to ensure that the provincial policy is rescinded or, alternatively, provide compensation to the complainant. The prospect of such a ruling would act as a deterrent to any measure to reverse the privatization of home care services.

It is also possible that a provincial government could decide to provide home care directly, as did the government of Manitoba in the early 1980s. In the Manitoba case, it was determined that home care could be provided better and more efficiently by government employees than by contracting to private agencies. The GATS monopolies rules (Article VIII) would obstruct any other provincial government which reaches the same conclusion. Another WTO member country could charge that public provision of home care constitutes an extension of a government monopoly to a service which was part of the commercial home care market covered by Canada's specific commitments. If such a challenge were successful, Canada would be required to negotiate compensation with other WTO members, or agree to an arbitration process, before implementing the new policy.[39] Again, the prospect of such a challenge would act as a deterrent to any government considering a policy to publicly provide home care services.

The Manitoba home care case is an instructive illustration of how the GATS not only restricts Canada's health policy options, but also imposes legally-enforceable private property rights which are at odds with Canadian legal norms.

In 1986, Home Orderly Services claimed its business had been confiscated by the Manitoba government decision to directly provide home care. The case was dismissed by a Manitoba Court and no compensation was awarded. In his decision in that case, Judge J. Scollin observed:

> *Government decisions of the sort in issue have serious private repercussions, but they are essentially political choices made with justifiable impunity in the public interest as perceived by the elected government... The reality was that the business existed at the sufferance of the taxpayer and at no time did the plaintiffs have a legal right to demand that the taxpayer should subsidize or even continue the services.*[40]

The Court's decision was upheld by the Manitoba Court of Appeal. In the Appeal Court ruling, Judge C.J.M. Monnin further observed:

> *Surely, after having provided the major portion of the income between 1969 and 1984, the government is not faced now with having to purchase as a going concern or having to substantially compensate what it has itself caused to be created by having hired the services of the plaintiff corporation.*[41]

Fifteen years later, commercial home care providers throughout Canada continue to rely almost entirely on public spending. But the extension of GATS coverage would provide them with a legal claim to ongoing public funding which was specifically dismissed by the Manitoba Courts in the Home Orderly Services case. The GATS monopolies rules (Article VIII) could require the government to negotiate compensation for any commercial operations which had previously provided home care services. Commercial home care agencies would effectively gain, through the GATS, a property right which is not recognized in Canadian law. This would constitute a powerful lever to obstruct the public interest which was so forcefully expressed by the Manitoba courts in the Home Orderly Services case.

Chapter 5
Conclusion and Recommendations

The commercial principles codified in the GATS are fundamentally incompatible with Canadian Medicare. As this report has shown, the GATS exemplifies a trade doctrine which construes many critical health policy measures as "non-tariff barriers" to trade in health services. Its single-minded fixation with expanding market access to all services directly conflicts with the values which underlie Canada's health care system, and which are expressed in the Canada Health Act.

Canada's health care system is facing enormous challenges, and there is virtually unanimous support for significant reform to the system. Although Canadians may not agree on the details of health care reform, there is overwhelming support for maintaining universal, publicly funded health care – as was demonstrated in the recent federal election. To do so, it is vital that we preserve our democratic capacity to consider and choose between different public policy options without fear of retaliation under international commercial treaties.

Former Health Minister Monique Begin has spoken eloquently about the fragility of the arrangements which support our health care system (see section 2.2 of this report). The present government can also look to the experience of Australia to be reminded of the need for precaution. During the past decade, the Australian health care system has been so undermined that 40 percent of Australians now depend on private health insurance and those who can't afford it are relegated to second-rate care at formerly pres-

tigious public teaching hospitals. A visiting epidemiologist
has this warning for Canadians:

> *Like many Australians, and I suspect, many Ca-*
> *nadians, I think that universal health cover is a*
> *good thing. But it's amazing how easily it can*
> *slip away if the government doesn't fund it and*
> *the population doesn't value it enough to notice*
> *and to argue the point.*[1]

With this warning in mind, Canada's representatives at
the GATS negotiations must exercise the utmost precaution, not the reckless enthusiasm they have displayed so
far.

The GATS and the Future of Health Care

Our report reinforces concerns that Canada's trade policy
is driven by narrow commercial interests which conflict
with the broader public interest in maintaining a universal, publicly funded health care system.

In section 2.3 we reviewed the federal government strategy for promoting exports of Canadian health services.
Based on highly questionable growth projections, the government's official strategy document focuses entirely on
expanding market access for Canadian telehealth services.
The "barriers to market entry" identified in this document
include regulatory measures designed to maintain professional standards; guard against malpractice and fraud; contain costs; and ensure patient privacy and confidentiality.

To identify these measures as "barriers to market access"
for Canadian telehealth exports is to target in other coun-

tries the public policy tools that Canadian governments rely on to maintain the integrity of our own health care system. As well as putting Canada in a questionable ethical position, this aggressive trade posture arguably conflicts with Canada's obligation under the International Covenant on Economic, Social and Cultural Rights to "respect the enjoyment of the right to health in other countries."

If this hypocritical agenda continues to influence Canada's negotiating objectives at the GATS, then Canadian demands will rebound, contributing to the dismantling of our own health care system. Even Canada's commercial health services corporations frankly acknowledge that there would be "a price to pay" for pursuing their export agenda.

The Canadian government must unequivocally affirm that safeguarding Canada's health care system will take precedence over securing market access for Canadian exports. It must disavow the dangerous illusion that Canada can gain access to other countries' markets for health services without ever granting access to the Canadian market in return.

The priority Canada gives to expanding markets for telehealth is of particular concern because telehealth applications cut across the full range of health care services. Any trade rules which apply to telehealth as a group could restrict how governments provide and regulate home care, diagnostic services, health information and other vital components of the our health care system. There is a danger that telehealth could be covered by GATS rules developed in the e-commerce negotiations which are being fast-tracked in the GATS 2000 negotiations.

The Canadian government should oppose any initiative to extend GATS coverage of telehealth services as a group, and it should ensure that the negotiations on ecommerce and telecommunications do not affect health services provided electronically or by other means.

Sections 3 and 4 of this report examined the health implications of the GATS. We found that federal government reassurances that health care will not be affected are highly misleading.

In fact, important features of our health care system are *already* exposed under existing GATS rules.

Health insurance is subject to the full force of GATS obligations, including the national treatment and market access rules, as well as most-favoured-nation and other general obligations. Not only did Canada list health insurance under the GATS; it inexplicably passed up the opportunity to explicitly shield public health insurance from GATS rules. These one-time chances to list limitations or to exempt public health insurance from the MFN rule are now irrevocably lost. Certain hospital and home care services may be similarly exposed to direct coverage due to the vagaries of the GATS classification system.

Most-favoured-nation and other general GATS rules likely apply already to most elements of our health care system. The record of WTO disputes and other technical interpretations indicate that Canadian health care services, which typically combine public financing with private delivery, would be considered within the scope of the GATS and therefore subject to its general obligations.

Given the high priority which Canadians attach to health care, Canadian negotiators' failure to take every available step to explicitly protect health services displays alarming carelessness, negligence or incompetence. The error in Canada's listing of health insurance is further evidence that our trade negotiators and their political masters have mishandled their responsibility to protect health care. Given this sorry record, Canadians should not trust current assurances that Medicare is fully safeguarded under the GATS.

The federal government's vocal insistence that public health care is not affected by the GATS appears to be founded mainly on a misplaced faith that it is excluded from the scope of the agreement. Article I.3 is, in fact, a highly qualified and very narrow exclusion which any sober analysis would find an extremely tenuous basis for protecting one of Canada's most significant social programs.

Experience at the WTO and in NAFTA shows that provisions which advance commercial interests will be interpreted in the most expansive manner while public interest exceptions will invariably be narrowly applied. Recent claims by leading WTO officials and by Canada's Ambassador to the WTO that health and social services are absolutely protected by article I.3 are at odds with a plain reading of the text and with the advice the WTO Secretariat provides to member nations. Canadians should be extremely skeptical of such reassurances, which will have little influence on the outcome of trade disputes or on the direction of future negotiations.

Action speaks louder than words. If the Government of Canada is genuinely commited to safeguarding our health care system, there are specific concrete steps which should be among our highest priorities in the GATS 2000 negotiations.

The Canadian government should conduct a systematic and comprehensive assessment of the health impacts of our commitments under the existing GATS agreement. In addition to considering the direct impacts on health care services such an assessment should consider the impacts on the determinants of health, which were briefly discussed in section 1.1

of this report. Among other things this would entail considering the implications of GATS obligations for health inequality, i.e., the distribution of health amongst different population groups within Canada and internationally.[2] Such an assessment should be made public and tabled in Parliament. It should also provide the basis for a public review of all future GATS provisions before they are ratified by Canada.

As mentioned above, close analysis does not support recent claims regarding the effectiveness of the Article I.3 exclusion for "services supplied in the exercise of governmental authority." *The Canadian government should raise the issue of the "governmental authority" exclusion during the GATS 2000 negotiations so that its meaning is clarified, and it is made fully effective. Amendments to this provision will be required to ensure that mixed public-private services, including health care, are fully excluded from the GATS.*

Given the significance of health care, it should not continue to be protected solely by definitional provisions which are subject to interpretation by other parties. *Canada should insist on a general exception for health care, which applies to all WTO members and will not be targeted in future rounds of negotiations, Because of the diversity of national health care systems, any such exception must be self-defining (as is the existing general exception for national security measures).*

Agreement on explicitly excluding health care from the scope of the agreement, either through amendments to Article I.3 or by means of a new general exception, should be a precondition for agreeing to any further commitments in the GATS 2000 negotiations.

Canada should also use every opportunity available to it to explicitly register its intention to shield health care from the GATS rules. In addition to excluding health care services from the scope of the agreement, our negotiators should enter explicit exceptions and limitations to all GATS commitments which may affect any health care services. While this will create some redundancy, it will make Canada's intentions absolutely clear to WTO trade panels and other WTO members. Their inexcusible failure to enter health-related exceptions and limitations to our existing GATS commitments raises concerns about whether Canada's trade negotiators are genuinely committed to shielding Canadian health care.

Special action is needed to safeguard Canada's ability to modify public health insurance in accordance with domestic policy priorities and without fear of provoking a GATS trade challenge. Canada has bound its GATS commitments in health insurance without entering any limitations for public health insurance. This means a decision to extend Medicare to cover prescription drugs or home care could be challenged by private health insurers who would lose commercial opportunities.

To safeguard our ability to revitalize Medicare, therefore, Canada must invoke GATS Article XXI to modify its schedule of specific commitments in health insurance. It must enter a limitation which explicitly shields public health insurance from these commitments. In order to preserve the ability to extend Medicare, Canada must also change the status of its commitments in commercial health insurance from "bound" to "unbound." This would remove the danger that private corporations could challenge future changes to Medicare which may affect their ability to provide commercial health insurance.

The federal government is acting recklessly by embarking on negotiations to extend and deepen the GATS without having first assessed the health care impacts of the existing agreement and secured the safeguards proposed above. The GATS 2000 negotiations mandate negotiations in a number of areas which may extend GATS coverage of health care services.

In the GATS 2000 negotiations, the Canadian government should make clear its opposition to extending coverage of health care services. It should:

- *oppose negotiations on rules regarding non-discriminatory domestic regulations, which would extend the reach of the GATS far into areas of domestic policy including health policy and working to eliminate the provisional application of the restrictions on domestic regulations contained in Article VI; and*

- *insist on maintaining the bottom-up features of the GATS, and oppose so-called "horizontal" negotiations which could extend GATS rules to health service by stealth, i.e., without requiring them to be positively listed.*

These recommendations are at odds with the federal government's commitment to extending and deepening the GATS, which Canadian officials pursue with an apparent disregard for the consequences. Our findings in this report, however, demonstrate that much greater precaution is needed to ensure that health care is protected as well as Canadians expect it to be. The above recommendations are practical steps which would give meaning to the assurances provided by the Prime Minister and other members of the federal government.

Beyond the GATS: Health as a Global Public Good

Safeguarding Canada's health care system requires firm international engagement, but in pursuit of a very different agenda than Canada's current trade policy. This agenda should not only ensure that trade agreements do not infringe upon the ability of citizens to democratically determine how they will support the health of their societies. It must also strengthen international mechanisms for addressing health issues that transcend national borders.

Research by numerous experts has shown the various ways in which health care services are different from market commodities.[3] The tragic consequences of treating health as a market commodity are most starkly evident in the AIDS pandemic in certain African countries. There, the TRIPS agreement has empowered multinational pharmaceutical firms to exercise private patent rights on products which were developed with enormous public funding, preventing South Africa and other nations from providing affordable treatment to reduce the death and suffering of their citizens. Our government's effort to "brand" Canadian health companies as "global health-keepers" is morally repugnant, given its recent dedication to opening markets for Canadian health- services exports by commodifying the provision of health care in other countries.[4]

Canada should join leading health experts and support concrete efforts to build international mechanisms for addressing health as a "global public good." This means ensuring that international collaboration to advance health is not obstructed by trade rules. As well as strengthening the capacities of the WHO and other international health organizations, Canada should commit itself to building a more balanced international order in which mechanisms for addressing the determinants of health – including income disparities, human rights and environmental conditions – are not superseded by the commercial interests advanced in trade agreements.

There has long been an evident need for collaboration among nations to monitor and control the spread of infectious disease. The international system of infectious disease surveillance, first established over a century ago, was a precursor of the World Health Organization.[5] Economic globalization has now given added prominence to the global public character of health, by internationalizing not only the agents that cause infectious diseases, but also the environmental and behavioural risks associated with non-infectious diseases, e.g., respiratory diseases, caused by air pollution, and cancers caused by tobacco consumption.

Chen et al. identify two forces through which health is becoming more of a global public good:

> *First, enhanced international linkages in trade, migration and information flows have accelerated the cross-border transmission of diesase and the international transfer of behavioural and environmental health risks. Second, intensified pressures on common-pool global resources of air and water have generated shared environmental threats. Globalization is not simply accelerating long-term trends but is ushering in contextual changes that are qualitatively and quantitatively different in disease risk, health vulnerability and policy resonse.[6]*

Canada should renew its heritage of enlightened internationalism by working to establish health as a global public good. Canada has been an international leader in the field of population health and health promotion. It has also played an important role in a number of innovative international legal instruments, including the Ottawa Treaty to Ban Anti-Personnel Landmines and the UN Convention on the Rights of the Child. This legacy should take precedence over narrow commercial interests in our approach to international health.

In a recent issues paper, the Canadian Society for International Health observes that:

> *A major challenge is to move global health policy relating to such issues as trade and health, food safety and security, women's rights and poverty alleviation, into other global policy organizations and arenas that have not traditionally been concerned with health, social and environmental issues. Many of the policy agreements to advance global health will need to be reached in organizations such as the World Trade Organization.*[7]

This is a big agenda and one that runs against Canada's orthodox trade policy. That orthodoxy, however, has been able to respond only defensively to the challenges posed by the failure of the WTO ministerial conference in Seattle.

A more far-sighted approach would involve trade policy specialists working in collaboration with experts in health and social policy to develop proposals for a more coherent international framework for addressing health as a global public good.

There are practical steps the Government of Canada can take to help initiate this ambitious agenda. The revision of the WHO International Health Regulations is one modest opportunity for Canada to advance global health. By supporting the competence of the WHO in determining legitimate health risks involved in WTO trade disputes, Canada would contribute to strengthening the enforcement of the International Health Regulations.[8]

The International Health Regulations (IHRs) are legally-binding rules requiring national governments to monitor and report outbreaks of certain designated diseases. National governments can be required to impose temporary trade restrictions and other measures to control the spread of a disease outbreak. Since 1995, the WHO has been working to update these regulations to make them more enforceable and to address the growing significance of new and re-emergent communicable diseases.

One impediment to enforcing the IHRs regulations is the loss of income from trade and tourism which can follow reports of an outbreak. This obstacle can be exacerbated when the IHRs conflict with member countries' WTO trade obligations to provide access to their national markets. The prospect of trade reprisals adds to the commercial pressures to avoid reporting a disease outbreak.

As part of its review, the WHO has proposed that the WTO Committee on Sanitary and Phytosanitary Measures (SPS) recognize WHO assessments of health risk, and that WTO enforcement powers be used to help back up the IHRs. Meaningful collaboration would require ceding to the WHO some of the authority which WTO trade panels currently assume for determining legitimate public health risks.[9] This would be a small step toward building an international framework for addressing health as a global public good.

Canada must also work on a larger canvas to support other nations in meeting the health needs of their citizens. It should support efforts to build a more balanced international economic order in which commercial interests no longer take precedence over human rights, environmental protection, income redistribution and other health-determining conditions.

In addition to strengthening the WHO and other international health organizations, Canada should support initiatives to counterbalance the authority of trade tribunals with more accountable forms of global governance. The primacy of human rights, including the right to health, should be assured in practice as well as in theory. To this end, Canada should support establishing a mechanism for resolving complaints of violations of nations' obligations under theInternational Covenant on Economic, Social and Cultural Rights.

The federal government should also review its export promotion and trade policies to ensure that they are consistent with its obligation under the Covenant to "respect the enjoyment of the right to health in other countries, and to prevent third parties violating the right in other countries..."[10]

These steps would bring Canada's international policies closer to our tarnished national self-image as an enlightened global citizen. They would also better support the values that underlie our health care system than is possible within the framework of the GATS agreement and the commercial principles which it advances.

Since the GATS agreement was concluded in 1994, it has been shrouded in secrecy and misinformation. As the federal government enters a new phase of GATS negotiations Canadians are now better informed – and more concerned — about its implications for health care and other vital services. This is due largely to the vigilance and dedication of individuals and organizations outside government. Continued public pressure – from providers of health services and from users of those services; from legislators, from public interest organizations and from the streets — will be needed to convince our government that the GATS must be fundamentally reformed.

Endnotes

Chapter 1

1   Jean Chrétien, *The Canadian Way in the 21st Century*, paper presented to the conference on Progressive Governance for the 21st Century, June 2-3 2000, Berlin Germany.

2   Several recent comparative studies examining the empirical associations between trade liberalization, growth and income distribution have reached conflicting conclusions. Rodriguez and Rodrik (2000), summarize the skeptical view; the view of leading proponents in presented in Dollar and Kray (2000) and in World Trade Organization, *Trade, Income Disparity and Poverty* (1999)

3   I am grateful to Diana Bronson of Rights and Democracy (Montreal) for guiding me to key documents to which this section refers.

4   United Nations, Committee on Economic, Social and Cultural Rights, General Comment No.14 E/C.12/2000/4 CESCR (4 July 2000), paragraph 9.

5   *Ibid*, paragraph 4.

6   Canada Health Act 1984, www.hc-sc.gc.ca .

7   Ibid, paragraphs 30-32.

8   *Ibid*, paragraph 39.

9   *Ibid*, paragraph 42.

10 United Nations Conference on Trade and Development, Trends in International Investment Agreements: An Overview, New York and Geneva: United Nations 1999 (UNCTAD/ITE/IIT/13), p.42.

11 OECD review of Spain, Sept 2000,p.219 (www..oecd.org/publications/e-book/4200051e.pdf).

12 World Health Organization, Health and Welfare Canada, Canadian Public Health Association, *Ottawa Charter for Health Promotion*, Ottawa: CPHA, 1986.

13 Federal, Provincial, Territorial Advisory Council on Population Health (ACPH), *Strategies for Population Health: Investing in the health of Canadians*, (Prepared for the meeting of the Ministers of Health, Halifax, September 14-151994), Health Canada.

14 ACPH, *Toward a Healthy Future: Second report on the health of Canadians 1999*, September 1999 Health Canada (www.hc-

sc.gc.ca) and Canadian Institute for Health Information (www.cihi.ca). This framework has been adopted as the structure for these recently initiated flagship reports.

[15] ACPH, *Toward a Healthy Future: Second report on the health of Canadians 1999*, September 1999 Health Canada (www.hc-sc.gc.ca) and Canadian Institute for Health Information (www.cihi.ca), p.3

[16] ACPH, Strategies, op. cit., p.33.

[17] "Global trade and health: key linkages and future challenges," in Bulletin of the World Health Organization, 2000, 78 (4) pp.521-534.

[18] Labonte, Ronald, Matthew Sanger, Nazeem Muhajarine and Sylvia Abonyi, "Globalization, Health and the New Liberalization Regime" in *Les Cahiers de l'IUED* (forthcoming).

Chapter 2

[1] Source: National Forum on Health, *The Public and Private Financing of Canada's Health System*, (September 1995). wwwnfh.hc-sc.gc.ca/publicat/public

[2] Canadian Institute for Health Information, *Health Care in Canada: a first annual report* (CIHI/Statistics Canada, 2000) p.19.

[3] CIHI, *The Evolution of Public and Private Health Care Spending in Canada, 1960 to 1997*, table 2, p.14. www.cihi.ca

[4] Ibid, table 5, p.28.

[5] Monique Bégin, "The Future of Medicare: recovering the Canada Health Act," The Justice Emmett Hall Memorial Lecture at the 8th Conference on Health Economics, Canadian Health Economics Research Association, University of Alberta, 20 August 1999.

[6] NFOH, op.cit. pp.6-7.

[7] All figures in the updated table are from Canadian Institute for Health Information, *Health Care in Canada: a first annual report (2000)*; and CIHI, *Evolution of Public and Private Health Care Spending*, op. cit., unless otherwise specified.

[8] Constitution Act 1982, article 36(2).

[9] Despite these pressures the Canadian health system is very cost efficient compared to the American system and compares favourably with European health systems. [XX add CIHI data on total and public health expenditures as % of GDP]

10   *Communiqué on Health*, First Ministers Meeting, Ottawa, September 11 2000.

11   Editorial, *CMAJ*, Sept 19 2000, 163 (6).

12   Quoted by Bégin, op.cit.

13   Monique Bégin, "The Future of Medicare: recovering the Canada Health Act," The Justice Emmett Hall Memorial Lecture at the 8th Conference on Health Economics, Canadian Health Economics Research Association, University of Alberta, 20 August 1999.

14   Roy Romanow, Notes for Remarks, Forum on Medicare – Sustainability and Accountability in the 21st Century, Vancouver May 11 2000.

15   Monique Bégin, "The Future of Medicare: recovering the Canada Health Act," The Justice Emmett Hall Memorial Lecture at the 8th Conference on Health Economics, Canadian Health Economics Research Association, University of Alberta, 20 August 1999.

16   Industry Canada, Trade Team Canada – Health Industries, *Health Industries: Canadian International Business Strategy (CIBS) 1999-2000* (strategis.ic.gc.ca/SSG/ht01211e.html). This paper sets out Canada's priorities for promoting health services exports. Unlike other sectors, there has been no public discussion paper on health services prepared for DFAIT's consultation on the GATS 2000 negotiations.

17   Legislation governing telehealth has recently been introduced in Norway and in Japan.

18   The CIBS forecast appears to be an error based on a private sector report which forecast total worldwide revenues of $839.144 *million* for telemedicine *products* and services. Telemedicine is a sub-category of telehealth, but this figure includes the value of trade in products as well as services. "World Market for Telemedicine Products and Services: Issues, Market Forecasts and Trends," Feedback Research Services Inc., June 1997. The author was unable to directly check this source due to its cost, and did not receive a reply to inquiries made to the Working Group on Health Services established for the DFAIT GATS 2000 consultations. Source for WTO data: www.wto.org/english/res_e/statis_e/j_e.htm.

19   Statistics Canada does not report data for trade in services. For a discussion of conceptual difficulties see: Guy Karsenty, "Assessing Trade in Services by Mode of Supply," in Pierre

Sauvé and Robert M. Stern (eds.), GATS 2000: new directions in services trade liberalization, Washington D.C.: Brookings, 2000, pp.33-56.

20 C IBS, op.cit., health services chapter, p.5.

21 DFAIT, Team Canada Market Research Centre and Canadian Trade Commissioner Service, *The Telemedicin/Telehealth Market in New England*, June 1999, p.5.

22 CIBS, op.cit., Introduction, p.3.

23 CIBS, op.cit., Health Services chaper, p.9.

24 Susan Harper (Director, Services Trade Policy Division, DFAIT) personal communication, 14 September 2000.

25 Colleen Fuller, Caring for Profit: how corporations are taking over Canada's health system, Ottawa and Vancouver: CCPA / New Star, 1998, p.246.

26 Information about the Coalition of Service Industries is available on its web site: www.usci.org. See also David Hartridge, "What the General Agreement on Trade in Services (GATS) Can Do," in Opening Markets for Banking World Wide, Proceedings of a Conference held in London, January 1997, cited in Scott Sinclair, GATS: How the World Trade Organization's new 'services' negotiations threaten democracy, Ottawa: CCPA, 2000, p.22.

27 Information about the International Summit on the Private Health Sector is available by Internet: http://www.aihs.com/summit/summitabout.html

28 Letter from Brian Harling, chair of the Medical and Health Care Products & Services SAGIT (Sectoral Advisory Group on International Trade) to the The Honourable Pierre Pettigrew, Minister of International Trade, 21 March 2000.

29 Industry Canada, Sector Competitiveness Framework Series: Telehealth Industry, Annex B (18 September 1998). strategis.ic.gc.ca/SSG/hs011329e.html.

30 CIBS, op. cit., Health Services chapter, p.10.

31 Bill Blaikie, An open letter to the Minister of International Trade, Hon. Pierre Pettigrew, September 21, 2000

Chapter 3

1 Much of the analysis in this chapter is drawn from Scott Sinclair, *GATS: How the World Trade Organization's new "services" nego-*

tiations threaten democracy), Ottawa: CCPA (2000). His book contains a fuller discussion of the issues summarized below.

2   WTO Secretariat, Trade in Services Division, *An Introduction to the GATS*, October 1999, p.1.

3   GATS article XXVIII

4   WTO Council for Trade in Services, *Health and Social Services: background note by the Secretariat*, S/C/W/50 (18 September 1998), paragraph 35.

5   Canada is a signatory to the WTO Agreement on Government Procurement, which is separate from the GATS and as a "plurilateral" agreement is optional for WTO members. The GPA covers procurement of certain services, but does not apply to provincial governments and their agencies.

6   WTO Secretariat, "Health and Social Services" op. cit., pp.18,28. Among the few countries that have listed MFN limitations, the majority of limitations concern bilateral agreements giving health professionals from each country preferential rights to practice in the other country.

7   William J. Drake and Kalypso Nicolaidïs, "Global Electronic Commerce and GATS: the millenium round and beyond," in Sauvé and Stern (eds.), pp.420-421.

8   See Scott Sinclair, op.cit., pp41ff. for more discussion of the implications of the EC Bananas case.

9   WTO Council for Trade in Services, *Health and Social Services: background note by the Secretariat*, 18 September 1998 (S/C/W/ 50), p.20.

10   WTO Council for Trade in Services, *Canada: Schedule of Specific Commitments* (15 April 1994) GATS/SC/16, pp.3-5,15.

11   Canada's limitation reads: "The supply of a service,or its subsidization, within the public sector is not in breach of this commitment" (i.e. to provide national treatment to listed services supplied by commercial presence). Ibid p.3

12   In addition to the commitments shown in the table, 76 WTO members (including Canada) have included health insurance in their schedules of specific commitments.

13   See for instance, "Frequently asked questions about health and education services" on the Services 2000 web site: strategis.gc.ca/SSG/sk00077e.html.

14   Susan Harper, Director, Services Trade Policy Division, DFAIT, presentation to Working Group of the Trade and Investment Research Project, Ottawa (14 September 2000).

15 In a recent ruling, the United Nations body responsible for classifications ruled that "on-line database publishing" of all kinds will be classified in "on-line information provision services" (CPC v.1 84300), a sub-class of Business Services. (See United Nations Classifications Registry, http://esa.un.org/unsd/cr/registry.) This ruling would seem to apply to many health information services which involve the assembly and storage of data from multiple sources and its distribution through electronic means.

16 Shaila Nijhowne (Statistics Canada) and David Usher (DFAIT), *Classification, the Measurement of Production and International Trade in Services, and GATS*, Paper presented to the Preparatory Conference, Services 2000: New Directions in Services Trade Liberalization, Washington D.C., June 1-2 1999, p.6.

17 This is the author's interpretation based on WTO discussion documents reviewed by Scott Sinclair, op cit. pp.75-81.

18 See discussion in Scott Sinclair, op.cit., pp.75-81.

19 Robert Ready (Director, International Investment and Services Policy, Industry Canada) and Vincent Sachetti (Canadian delegate to the Working Party on Domestic Regulation), presentation to the Trade and Investment Research Project, Ottawa, 14 September 2000.

20 WTO Secretariat, Trade in Services Division, *GATS Article VI.4: disciplines on domestic regulation applicable to all services*, S/C/W/96, March 1 1999.

21 See Scott Sinclair, op. cit., pp.85-89.

Chapter 4

1 The official government view on this issue is unknown as it is not discussed in any public documents. On two occassions the author made direct inquiries to senior officials with responsibility for this file. No substantive response was provided in either case.

2 GATS, article VII

3 WTO, Trade in Services, *Canada: Schedule of Specific Commitments, supplement 4*, (26 February 1998) GATS/SC/16/Suppl.4. This revision includes changes related to further liberalisation of banking services to allow foreign banks to establish branches in Canada.

4   Expansion of GATS coverage to include cross-border trade and domestic regulations is explicitly contemplated in the GATS Financial Services Agreement, which is considered to establish a baseline for the GATS 2000 negotiations. Financial services were the subject of separate WTO negotiations, concluding in December 1997 with the Financial Services Agreement which came into force 1 March 1999. This agreement binds Canada and other nations to maintain the level of openness for financial services providers which prevailed in 1997. In addition some countries, including Canada, made further commitments to liberalisation in banking services. Canada's health insurance commitments were not affected by these subsequent negotiations.

5   Canada's specific commitments are consistent with the WTO "Understanding on Commitments in Financial Services", concluded at the same time as the GATS 1994. Articles 3 and 4 of this Understanding limit national treatment and market access rules for financial services provided by cross-border supply and by consumption abroad to certain forms of maritime and transportation insurance, (and to banking services consumed abroad). There is no such limitation for national treatment and market access rules on financial services provided through commercial presence (article 5).

6   Also significant is a standstill provision included in the WTO Understanding on Commitments in Financial Services, and reaffirmed in the schedule of financial services commitments Canada submitted pursuant to the WTO Financial Sevices Agreement. This provision (section A of the Understanding) restricts any limitations on Canada's commitments to existing non-conforming measures. In other words, new government measures cannot be shielded by any of the limitations Canada has entered into its schedule.

7   A revised version of the CPC (CPC v.1) changes the classification for health insurance (to 71320) and excludes insurance for hospital and medical expenses covered by public health insurance. This revised classification, however, has not been adopted by the WTO and the CPC provisional system remains the operative classification for the purposes of interpreting Canada's GATS scheduling commitments. The classification systems referred to are both maintained by the United Nations Statistics Division: United Nations, Provisional Central Product Clas-

sification 1991 (ST/ESA/STAT/SER.M/77); and United Nations Central Product Classification version 1.0 (ST/ESA/STAT/SER.M/77/Ver.1.0) 1998. Both can be accessed through the United Nations web site: http://www.un.org/Depts/unsd/class/family.htm.

8   Canada inadvertently listed wholesale trade in motor vehicles by entering the CPC classification for this service in the "retail services" section of the Canadian GATS schedule. Despite this discrepancy, and despite arguments that Canada did not intend to make specific commitments in this area, the WTO panel ruled that wholesale trade of motor vehicles is covered. See, Sinclair, op cit, pp.52-53.

9   WTO, Trade in Services, *Canada: Schedule of Specific Commitments, supplement 4,* (26 February 1998) GATS/SC/16/Suppl.4. It is noteworthy that the schedule includes limitations to permit provincial government monopoly provision of auto insurance in Manitoba and British Columbia, but no limitations related to provincial health insurance plans.

10   GATS, *Canada: List of Article II (MFN) Exemptions,* 15 April 1994 GATS/EL/16; and *Canada: List of Article II (MFN) Exemptions, supplement 1* 28 July 1995, GATS/EL/16/suppl.1; and *Canada: List of Article II (MFN) Exemptions, supplement 2,* 26 February 1998, GATS/EL/16/suppl.2. The Financial Services Agreement permitted WTO members a one-time-only opportunity to re-open their schedule of MFN commitments in order to enter new limitations.

11   The GATS Annex on Financial Services broadens the definition of "services provided in the exercise of governmental authority" but maintains the criterion that there be no competition with commercial service providers (Annex article 1(b) and 1(c)). It appears that Canada considers public health insurance to be excluded under the GATS Article 1.3(b) definition, rather than the expanded Annex definition, because it has not listed provincial health insurance plans among existing financial services monopolies as required by the monopoly rights provision of the Understanding on Commitments in Financial Services (article 1). This interpretation is reinforced by the fact that Canada did list a limitation for monopoly provision of auto insurance in Manitoba and British Columbia.

12   *Annex on Financial Services,* article 5

13   GATS articles VIII.4 and XXI.2, XXI.3 and XXI.4.

14 See, for instance: "WCB will pay to move workers to top of surgery lists," The Vancouver Sun (September 14 1998). This practice, and the predatory interest commercial insurers have shown in the market for rehabilitation care, has led Colleen Fuller to call Workers' Compensation "the Achilles heel of Canada's health care system" (Caring for Profit, page 173).

15 Salah H. Mandil discusses the potential telehealth provides for for expanding managed care operations in "Telehealth: What is it? Will it propel cross-border trade in health services?" in Zarilli and Kinnon op. cit., pp.79 to 110.

16 Finance Canada, Consultation Paper for the World Trade Organization Negotiations on Financial Services, 2000. www.fin.gc.ca/gats/wto2000_1e.html.

17 Salah H. Mandil discusses the potential telehealth provides for for expanding managed care operations in "Telehealth: What is it? Will it propel cross-border trade in health services?" in Zarilli and Kinnon op. cit., pp.79 to 110.

18 Finance Canada, op cit.

19 CPCprov code 93110. In CPC v.1 this definition has been revised to more precisely enumerate the medical services included in "hospital services".

20 CPCprov. Code 87403. Other components of CPC 874 include "disinfecting and exterminating services", "window cleaning services" and "other building cleaning services".

21 Canada's entry for hotels and restaurants references CPC codes 641 (hotels and other lodging services), 642 (food serving services), and 643 (beverage serving services for consumption on the premises). "Food serving services" includes: "meal serving services with self-service facilities" (CPC 6422) and "caterer services, providing meals outside" (CPC 6423).

22 A few small for-profit hospitals were in operation prior to the creation of Medicare and have been permitted to continue providing very specific insured services. For instance the Shouldice Clinic in Toronto, which offers hernia operations, was grandparented as a for-profit hospital under the Ontario *Private Hospitals Act* (1973).

23 The Health Care Protection Act, introduced in March 2000, is awaiting proclamation by the Government of Alberta. The category of "approved surgical facilities" created by the Act conforms with the GATS definition of hospitals, which rests on the presence of nursing care.

24 Canadian Union of Public Employees, *Cooking Up a Storm: shared food services in the health care sector* (March 1996); and *Cooking Up a Storm: Part II* (June 1998).

25 Article XVII

26 Steven Shrybman, "A Legal Opinion Concerning NAFTA Investment and Services Disciplines and Bill 11: Proposals by Alberta to privatize the delivery of certain insured health care services," February 2000 (available from the Canadian Union of Public Employees, www.cupe.ca/issues/healthcare.) The federal government has refused to release its legal review of this issue.

27 Article VI. Although this article is grouped with the GATS general rules its most consequential requirements currently apply only to listed services. Expanded coverage of these rules appears to have been contemplated by the placement of Article VI, and the sweeping mandate it sets for negotiations. See section 3.2.2 for more discussion.

28 Article XV. See section 3.2.3 for more discussion.

29 Paul Leduc Brown reviews definitions of home care in *Unsafe Practice: restructuring and privatization in Ontario Health Care*, Canadian Centre for Policy Alternatives 2000, pp. 81-2.

30 Peter Coyte (University of Toronto), "Home Care in Canada: passing the buck," May 2000. A 1998 Health Canada report estimates that public spending on home care was $2.1 billion in 1997-98. Estimates of homecare spending are complicated by difficulties in accounting for uncompensated care by family members, and difficulties in distinguishing between spending on health and spending on household consumption.

31 WTO, Services Sectoral Classification List (MTN.GNS/W/120, 10 July 1991).

32 CPCprov code 93191: "deliveries and related services, nursing services, physiotherapeutic and para-medical services". (Cpc v.1 adds some clarification to the description, including "These services are provided by authorised persons, other than medical doctors.") It should be noted that, unlike the GATS, the CPC groups this category within the health services sector.

33 Article XIII includes a temporary exception for government procurement, and a commitment to negotiations. See section 3.2.2 of this paper.

34 Sinclair, op cit, p.81.

35 NAFTA Chapter 10, Article 1001 5(a)

36   Sinclair, op. cit., p. 90.
37   Shelly Jamieson, President of Extendicare Canada, remarks at conference on Private-Public Partnerships, November 2000.
38   See Paul Leduc Browne, op. cit., pp.81-132 for a detailed analysis of the Ontario experience with privatized home care services.
39   GATS articles VIII.4 and XXI.2, XXI.3 and XXI.4.
40   *Home Orderly Services et al. v. Government of Manitoba* (1986), 32 D.L.R. (4th) p.758.
41   *Home Orderly Services et al. v. Government of Manitoba* (1987), 43 D.L.R. (4th) p.365.

Chapter 5

1   Alexandra Barrett, "A heads up from down under," *Ottawa Citizen*, 18 November 2000 p.A19
2   Canadian Society for International Health, *Issue Paper on Economic Globalization, Trade Liberalization, Governance and Health*, November 2000.
3   See for instance, the articles in Daniel Drache and Terry Sullivan (eds.), *Health Reform: Public Success, Private Failure*, Routledge, 1999.
4   "Promoting these companies as global healthkeepers, which are positioned to meet the challenges of the 21st century, is the underlying theme that drives this international business strategy," from the *Canadian International Business Strategy (CIBS) for Health Industries 1999-2000*, introduction p.4 (Industry Canada, strategis.ic.ca/SSG.ht01208e.html).
5   Mark W. Zacher, "Global Epidemiological Surveillance: international collaboration to monitor infectious diseases", in Kaul, Grunberg, Stern eds, *Global Public Goods: international cooperation in the 21st Century*, UNDP 1999.
6   Lincoln C. Chen, Tim G. Evans and Richard A. Cash, "Health as a Global Public Good," in Kaul et al (eds.) op cit., p289.
7   CSIH, *op cit.*, p.21.
8   Supporting the competence of the WHO is this matter would also contribute to counterbalancing a damaging implication of the WTO panel ruling in the Asbestos case, in which the Panel arrogated to itself the competence to determine whether asbestos products pose a public health risk.

9   Committee on Sanitary and Phytosanitary Measures, "Global Crises – Global Solutions: Managing urgent international public health events with the revised International Health Regulations," Information paper submitted by the World Health Organization (G/SPS/GEN/179, 31 May 2000); and Mark W. Zacher, "Global Epidemiological Surveillance: international collaboration to monitor infectious diseases", in Kaul, Grunberg, Stern eds, *Global Public Goods: international cooperation in the 21st Century*, UNDP 1999.

10   United Nations Committee on Economic, Social and Cultural Rights, *General Comment 14* (E/C 12/2000/4), 4 July 2000, paragraph 39.

Bibliography

Armstrong P and Armstrong H, *Wasting Away: the undermining of Canadian health care*, Toronto: Oxford University Press, 1996.

Bégin, Monique, *The Future of Medicare: Recovering the Canada Health Act*, Canadian Centre for Policy Alternatives (originally presented as The Justice Emmett Hall Memorial Lecture at the 8th Conference on Health Economics, Canadian Health Economics Research Association, health at the University of Alberta, 20 August 1999).

Bertrand, Agnes and Laurence Kalafatides, *The WTO and Public Health*, The Ecologist, 29(6): 365-368.

Bettcher and Yach, *The globalization of public health ethics?* Millenium: Journal of International Studies 1998, 27(3), 469-496.

Bettcher, Yach, Guindon, *Global trade and health: key linkages and future challenges*, Bulletin of the World Health Organization, 2000 (78,4) pp521-534.

Brown, Paul Leduc, *Unsafe Practice: restructuring and privatization in Ontario Health Care*, Canadian Centre for Policy Alternatives 2000. Canada, Office of the Prime Minister, *The Canadian Way in the 21st Century*, paper presented to informal heads of government meeting on Progressive Governance for the 21st Century, Berlin 2-3 June 2000.

Canadian Institute for Health Information and Statistics Canada, *Health Indicators 2000* (www.cihi.ca) May 2000.

Canadian Institute for Health Information and Statistics Canada, *Health Care in Canada: A first annual report*, (www.cihi.ca) May 2000.

Canadian Institute for Health Information, *The Evolution of Public and Private Health Care Spending 1960 to 1997*, (www.cihi.ca) (no date). Canadian Public Health Association, *Focus on Health: public health in health services restructuring*, board of directors issue paper, February 1996.

Canadian Society for International Health, *Issue Paper on Economic Globalization, Trade Liberalization, Governance and Health*, November 2000.

Chen LC, Evans TG, Cash RA, *Health as a Global Public Good*, in Kaul I, Grunberg I, Stern MA eds, *Global Policy Goods: international cooperation in the 21ˢᵗ century*, New York: Oxford University Press, 1999.

Committee on Sanitary and Phytosanitary Measures, "Global Crises – Global Solutions: Managing urgent international public health events with the revised International Health Regulations," Information paper submitted by the World Health Organization (G/SPS/GEN/179, 31 May 2000)

Dollar, D. and Kraay, A. (2000) *Growth is Good for the Poor.* Washington: World Bank. (www.worldbank.org/research).

Drache D and Sullivan T eds, *Health Reform: public success, private failure*, New York: Routledge 1999.

Drake, William and Kalypso Nicolaidïs, "Global Electronic Commerce and GATS: the millenium round and beyond," in Sauvé and Stern (eds.),

Drager N., *Making trade work for public health: WTO talks in Seattle offer an opportunity to get public health on the trade agenda*, British Medical Journal , 1999, 319:1214-1214.

European Commission, *Communication on Precautionary Principle*, Brussels 2 February 2000 (europa.eu.int/comm/trade).

Evans, Barer, Lewis, Rachlis, Stoddart, *Private Highway, One-Way Street: The Deklein and Fall of Canadian Medicare?* Centre for Health Services and Policy Research, University of British Columbia, March 2000.

Federal, Provincial and Territorial Advisory Committee on Population Health (ACPH), *Toward a Healthy Future: Second report on the health of Canadians,* (www.hc-sc.gc.ca) September 1999.

Federal, Provincial and Territorial Advisory Committee on Population Health (ACPH), *Statistical Report on the Health of Canadians*, (www.hc-sc.gc.ca) September 1999.

Federal, Provincial, Territorial Advisory Committee on Population Health (ACPH), Working Group on Healthy Child Development, *Investing in Early Child Development: the health sector contribution*, paper prepared for the Conference of Federal/Provincial/Territorial Ministers of Health, Charlottetown, PEI 16-17 September 1999.

Federal, Provincial, Territorial Advisory Council on Population Health (ACPH), *Strategies for Population Health: Investing in the health of Canadians*, (Prepared for the meeting of the Ministers of Health, Halifax, September 14-151994), Health Canada.

Fuller, Colleen, *Caring for Profit: how corporations are taking over Canada's health system*, Ottawa and Vancouver: New Star Books and Canadian Centre for Policy Alternatives, 1998.

Hartridge, David (Director of Trade in Services, WTO Secretariat) unpublished letter to Mike Waghorne (Assistant General Secretary, Public Services International), 31 May 2000.

Industry Canada, *Canadian International Business Strategy (CIBS) for Health Industries 1999-2000*, (strategis.ic.ca/SSG.ht01208e.html).

Karsenty, Guy "Assessing Trade in Services by Mode of Supply," in Pierre Sauvé and Robert M. Stern (eds.).

Koivusalo M and Ollila E, *Making a Healthy World: agencies, actors and policies in international health*, New York and Helsinki: Zed Books and STAKES, 1997.

Koivusalo, Meri, *World Trade Organisation and Trade-Creep in Health and Social Policies*, (Globalism and Social Policy Programme, University of Sheffield and STAKES, National Research and Development Centre for Welfare and Health, Helsinki) GASPP Occasional Papers no 4/1999.

Labonte, Ronald, Matthew Sanger, Nazeem Muhajarine and Sylvia Abonyi, "Globalization, Health and the New Liberalization Regime" in *Les Cahiers de l'IUED* (forthcoming).

Labonte, Ronald, *Brief to the World Trade Organization: World Trade and Population Health* (submitted on behalf of the Canadian Public Health Association and the International Union for Health Promotion and Education), 8 November 1999.

National Forum on Health, *Canada Health Action: Building on the Legacy (final report volume I)*, Ottawa: Minister of Public Works and Government Services, February 1997.

National Forum on Health, *Canada Health Action: Building on the Legacy (synthesis reports and issues papers, final report volume II)*, Ottawa: Minister of Public Works and Government Services, February 1997.

Nijhowne, Shaila (Statistics Canada) and David Usher (DFAIT), *Classification, the Measurement of Production and International Trade in Services, and GATS*, Paper presented to the Preparatory Conference, Services 2000: New Directions in Services Trade Liberalization, Washington D.C., June 1-2 1999.

Pollock, A. and Price, D. (2000) "Re-writing the regulations: How the World Trade Organisation could accelerate privatisation in health-care systems," *The Lancet*, 356:1995-2000 (December 9 2000).

Price, David, Allyson Pollock and Jean Shaoul, How the World Trade Organisation is shaping domestic policies in health care, The Lancet, vol.354:1889-1892 (November 27 1999).

Public Services International (Dain Bolwell), *Great Expectations: the future of trade in services*, draft July 2000
Registered Nurses Association of Ontario, *Submission to the DFAIT consultations on the General Agreement on Trade in Services (GATS)*, Toronto, June 29 2000.

Rodriguez, F. and Rodrik, D. (2000) *Trade Policy and Economic Growth: A Skeptic's Guide to the Cross-National Evidence*, University of Maryland and Harvard University.

Romanow, Roy, *Notes for Remarks* at the Forum on Medicare – Sustainability and Accountability in the 21st Century, Vancouver 11 May 2000.

Sauve, Pierre and Robert Stern eds., *GATS 2000: New Directions in Services Trade Liberalization,* Brookings Feb.2000

Sinclair, Scott *GATS: Hhow the World Trade Organization's new "services" negotiations threaten democracy,* Ottawa: Canadian Centre for Policy Alternatives (2000).

Stephensen, Sherry ed., *Services Trade in the Western Hemisphere: Liberalization, Integration and Reform,* Brookings June 2000

Stephenson, Sherry M., *The State of the FTAA Negotiations at the turn of the Millenium,* paper prepared for the Conference on Trade and Western Hemisphere, organized by Southern Methodist University, Dallas, 25 March 2000.

Swenarchuk, Michelle, *The Cartagena Biosafety Protocol: Opportunities and Limitations,* (www.web.net/cela/Trade&Env/biosafe.htm) February 2000.

United Nations, *International Covenant on Economic, Social and Cultural Rights* (entered into force 3 January 1976), www.unhchr.ch/html/menu3/b/a_cescr.htm.

United Nations Children's Fund, Innocenti Research Centre, *A League Table of Child Poverty in Rich Countries,* (Innocenti report card issue no.1, June 2000).

United Nations Committee on Economic, Social and Cultural Rights, *General Comment 14* (E/C 12/2000/4), 4 July 2000.

Warner D., *NAFTA and trade in medical services between the US and Mexico,* Austin TX, University of Texax at Austin, 1997.

World Health Organization, "Revision of the International Health Regulations – Progress Report, July 2000" in the WHO *Weekly Epidemiological Record* v.75, no.29: 233-240 (21 July 2000) www.who.int/wer.

World Health Organization, Task Force on Health Economics, *Health Economics – Technical Briefing Note – Measuring trade liberalization against public health objectives: the case of health sevices*, Geneva 1997.

World Health Organization, Health and Welfare Canada, Canadian Public Health Association, *Ottawa Charter for Health Promotion*, Ottawa: CPHA, 1986.

World Trade Organization (1999) *Trade, Income Disparity and Poverty*. Special Study 5.

World Trade Organization, Committee on Sanitary and Phytosanitary Measures, *Global Crises – Global Solutions: Managing urgent international public health events with the revised international health regulations* (information paper submitted by the World Health Organization) (G/SPS/GEN179), 31 May 2000

World Trade Organization, Council for Trade in Services, Health and Social Services: *Background note* by the Secretariat, S/C/W/50, 18 September 1998

WTO Council for Trade in Services, *Canada: Schedule of Specific Commitments* (15 April 1994) GATS/SC/16

WTO Secretariat, Trade in Services Division, *GATS Article VI.4: disciplines on domestic regulation applicable to all services*, S/C/W/96, March 1 1999.

WTO, Secretariat, Trade in Services Division, *An Introduction to the GATS*, October 1999 (available on WTO web site).

Yach and Bettcher, *The globalization of public health (I and II)*, American Journal of Public Health, 1998, 88 pp.735-8, 738-41.

Zacher, Mark W. "Global Epidemiological Surveillance: international collaboration to monitor infectious diseases", in Kaul, Grunberg, Stern eds, *Global Public Goods: international cooperation in the 21st Century*, UNDP 1999.

Zarilli, Simonetta and Colette Kinnon (eds.), International Trade in Health Services: A development perspective, jointly issued by the United Nations Conference on Trade and Development and the World Health Organization, (UNCTAD/ITCD;TS B/5; WHO/ TFHE/98.1) 1998.